"Here we learn that to attempt to recuperate an erased past is an obsessive task, following faint threads into places of memorial, tragic time, aging bodies—the fissures, gaps, and scars of which can never be fulfilled. In the void between, ghosts emerge and disappear as dreams. A photograph on a wall in an obscure museum in an old Montana fort of layered imprisonments becomes our ghost-guide, its playful enigmatic gaze the journey's beginning. In a weaving meditation, Brandon Shimoda pens an elegant eulogy for his grandfather Midori, yet also for the living, we who survive on the margins of graveyards and rituals of our own making."—**Karen Tei Yamashita**, author of *Letters to Memory*

"If someone asked me what a poet's history might look and read like, I would say Brandon Shimoda's *The Grave on the Wall*. It is part dream, part memory, part forgetting, part identity. It is a remarkable exploration of how citizenship is forged by the brutal US imperial forces—through slave labor, forced detention, indiscriminate bombing, historical amnesia and wall. If someone asked me, where are you from? I would answer, from *The Grave on the Wall*."—**Don Mee Choi**, author of *Hardly War*

"In *The Grave on the Wall*, Brandon Shimoda has conceived a moving monument to his grandfather Midori made not of stone but of fractured memories and dreams, fairy tales and family photographs, pilgrimages to alien enemy internment camps, burial grounds, deserts, and the Inland Sea, all bound together by lambent strands of ancestral and immigrant histories. Within this haunted sepulcher built out of silence, loss, and grief—its walls shadowed by the traumas of racial oppression and violence—a green river lined with peach trees flows beneath a bridge that leads back to the grandson. To read this astounding grave on the wall, to peel back the wall's layers of meaning, reveals less a finished portrait of 'the man made of ash' than a rippling representation of the related forces at play that shape the grandfather's absence."—**Jeffrey Yang**, author of *Hey, Marfa: Poems*

"In *The Grave on the Wall*, Bran
grandfath

WIT
ESTES
LIBF

that untold debt we all owe our forebears to whom we owe, if not the ordinary dailiness of lives, then at least basic facts of our existence. The legacy of past generations—though we embody them in some way, so often unknowingly replicate their gestures, tones of voices or facial expressions, maybe the curl of a lock of hair—that inheritance so often goes untold, except that Brandon Shimoda begins here accounting for it, beyond the borders of memory and forgetting, beyond the known and unknown. Shimoda intercedes into the absences, gaps and interstices of the present and delves the presence of mystery. This mystery is part of each of us. Shimoda outlines that mystery in silence and silhouette, in objects left behind at site-specific travels to Japan and in the disparate facts of his grandpa's FBI file. Gratitude to Brandon Shimoda for taking on the mystery which only literature accepts as the basic challenge."—**Sesshu Foster**, author of *City of the Future*

"Brandon Shimoda's *The Grave on the Wall* begins with a sentence that cannot be read. Impossible writing: 'My grandfather had one memory of his childhood in Hiroshima: washing the feet of his grandfather's corpse.' This is a book that can't be repaired or remembered, but which conjoins itself to subluminous modes of loss in possible readers. Shimoda is a mystic writer. He puts what breaches itself (always) onto the page, so that the act of writing becomes akin to paper-making: an attention to fibers, coagulation, texture and the water-fire mixtures that signal irreversible alteration or change. Does this book end? Is there a sentence that closes it? Or does it keep being written and forgotten then written again, each time a reader opens it (the book) for the first time? I have never met this writer in person, and perhaps I never will, but he has written a book that touches the bottom of my own soul."—**Bhanu Kapil**, author of *Ban en Banlieue*

"Sometimes a work of art functions as a dream. At other times, a work of art functions as a conscience. In the tradition of Juan Rulfo's *Pedro Páramo*, Brandon Shimoda's *The Grave on the Wall* is both. It is also the type of fragmented reckoning only America could instigate."—**Myriam Gurba**, author of *Mean*

# THE GRAVE ON THE WALL

# THE GRAVE ON THE WALL

Brandon Shimoda

City Lights Books | San Francisco

Library of Congress Cataloging-in-Publication Data
Names: Shimoda, Brandon, author.
Title: The grave on the wall / Brandon Shimoda.
Description: San Francisco : City Lights Books, [2019] | Includes
  bibliographical references and index.
Identifiers: LCCN 2019015708 (print) | LCCN 2019020566 (ebook) | ISBN
  9780872867932 | ISBN 9780872867901 (alk. paper)
Subjects: LCSH: Shimoda, Midori 1911-1996. | Shimoda, Brandon—Family. |
  Japanese Americans—Biography. | Japanese American
  photographers—Biography. | Immigrants—United States—Biography. |
  Japanese Americans—Evacuation and relocation, 1942-1945. | Grandfathers.
  | Grandparent and child.
Classification: LCC E184.J3 (ebook) | LCC E184.J3 S47 2019 (print) | DDC
  973/.04956—dc23
LC record available at https://lccn.loc.gov/2019015708

City Lights Books are published at the City Lights Bookstore
261 Columbus Avenue, San Francisco, CA 94133
www.citylights.com

*for my great-great-grandmother, Yumi Taguchi*

*and my daughter, Yumi Taguchi*

# CONTENTS

Subject stated he thinks Japan is "Hell." Subject stated, "I don't want to go back to Japan and I wish that they would give me a gun to go and fight Japan."

Subject's appearance is due to possession of camera. He is physically frail, of an artistic and very sensitive nature. He is high strung. He had difficulty restraining tears. He feels discouraged. He came to America when he was nine. He states it is difficult for him to look at himself as an alien . . . Certainly none of his conduct bears a remote relation to anything subversive . . . He represents one of the many individual tragedies of the war . . . We recommend that he is paroled under sponsorship as soon as possible so that his spirit may not be broken.

As a result of my contacts with this man, I am convinced that he has a plan in mind to do something which may be harmful to the country or the people in it and have been thoroughly satisfied to have him interned, and for that reason I do not believe that he should be allowed on his own until we know more about what was impelling his wilful [*sic*] violation of orders.

1128762

## THE PERIOD OF SUMMONING RELATIVES

My grandfather had one memory of his childhood in Hiroshima: washing the feet of his grandfather's corpse. He was six or five or four. He stood in the doorway of the room where his grandfather's corpse had been prepared. His grandfather, covered in a white towel and lying on a thin futon in the middle of the room, looked like he was sleeping. There was a sponge in a large white bowl of lucid water, and a robe, tightly folded, in the corner. My grandfather's mother and three older brothers nodded at him to enter.

*He looks like he is dreaming.*

He studied his mother and brothers before kneeling beside them. He touched one of his grandfather's feet. The first touch was the most daunting. The vein. He was afraid it might come apart in his hand. The skin was the texture of the rooms in which he spent time with his grandfather. But the seasons had been extinguished. He sank the sponge in the water, wrung it out, and touched it, tentatively, to his grandfather's sole.

*Like he is dreaming us into the room with him, washing his body. Dreaming my thoughts, even; that I think he is dreaming.*

He knew his grandfather was dead. His brothers told him. How did they know? A bead of water sank into the tatami.

He had a dream about a woman being lured from deep inside a cave to its mouth, where a mirror hung from a branch and was burning. A grandfather is a strange, somewhat impossible work of conscience, especially when old, especially when in a state of decline, on the verge of appearing to dream.

My grandfather's name is Midori Shimoda. He was born on an island off the coast of Hiroshima. He was born three years in a row, 1909, 1910, 1911, depending on whose memory is being consulted. According to my grandmother, June Shimoda, he was born March 26, 1911. According to records kept by the FBI—the file opens April 7, 1942—he was born a year earlier, March 26, 1910. According to a biography accompanying an exhibition of early-twentieth-century Japanese American photography at the Japanese American National Museum in Los Angeles, he was born a year before that, March 26, 1909.[1] His death, after nearly two decades with Alzheimer's, unfolded across a number of years, the final year being 1996. He died in the United States. He had long forgotten the island, its name, that he was born there. It had been eighty years since he left the village of Oko, stepped off Kurahashi onto a boat to cross the Ondo Strait to Honshu. Eighty years since he moved, with his mother and three older brothers, to Nakanose, in Kumamoto, where his father was from, where his grandmother (his father's mother), Yumi Taguchi, had prepared space in her house. That is where he lived before immigrating to the United States. He returned to Japan only once, in 1983. Japan was, by then, as much a curiosity—changeless, always changing, filled with faces assumed yet uncanny—as it was his birthplace and ancestral homeland.

---

1. *Making Waves: Japanese American Photography, 1920–1940*, February-June 2016.

Midori was nine when he left Japan. He was in his seventies when he returned. Not only had the homeland changed, but most of the places he visited (Kamakura, Kyoto, Miyajima, Nagoya, Takayama), he was visiting for the first time. Land, not home, maybe not even land. The *maybe not even land* in which he was most likely to encounter his ancestors—whether they were home or not—were in Nakanose and Oko. He did not visit either of them.

I visited Nakanose the summer of my thirty-third year. I visited Oko the summer of my thirty-eighth year. No one in my family had visited either place in almost one hundred years. Nakanose no longer exists. Oko is on the edge of extinction. I went to where Nakanose once was, and to Oko, to visit Midori, but within a basic confusion. The grandfather I had in mind was old; if I was seeking him there, I would have to be seeking a child.

Kure is thirty minutes by train from downtown Hiroshima. Kurahashi is twenty minutes by bus from downtown Kure. Katsuragahama is thirty minutes by bus from the Ondo Bridge, spiraled on both ends, bright red. It is the closest town of any size to Oko. Katsuragahama has hot springs, a shipbuilding museum, an inn, a beach, and, between the beach and the road, a grove of five hundred pine trees. In the seventh or eighth century, a poet sat beneath the pines and, facing the sea, wrote an ode. To the pines, to what he felt to be their perfection. The ode enfolded a lamentation on what the poet felt, by comparison, to be his perilously misshapen life. The pines held the sound of the waves and the poet's silent labor. The poem is one of the many thousands of poems in the *Man'yoshu* (Collection of Ten Thousand Leaves) and is inscribed on the face of a large stone that sleeps beneath the pines. The day I arrived, it was raining. The poem and its characters were leaking.

I asked Natsuko, the innkeeper, about Oko. Did it exist? (I was afraid it did not exist.) *It exists*, she said, *yes, but there is little reason to go.* We were standing on the stairs beside a window looking onto the pines. Then she said, *I went there once . . . It is famous for its sunrises.* I marveled at the thought of a place giving birth to its own suns, separate from those of the rest of the world.

The bus from Katsuragahama to Oko does not run very often. It is very small. White, shaped like a loaf of bread. Lisa and I were the only people on the bus. The driver was formal. He did not look up once into his mirror. I imagined him announcing the names of the stops to an empty bus. The road followed the coast, people fishing off white rocks, with children, radios, plastic bottles of tea. The bus passed into trees, bamboo. Then back into the open. The driver announced Oko. The stop was four wooden school chairs lined up against a wooden building facing the harbor.

Oko is arranged up the side of a foothill at the base of a range of small mountains. The predominant color—gunpowder gray—is set by the ceramic roof tiles. The houses are a combination of light blue and burned wood. Above the houses are trees, dark green, to the top of the mountain, with the occasional granite exposure. The village comes right up to the sea, separated by a narrow road and a seawall.

It was mid-afternoon. The village was at peace. A canal ran along its western edge. Green weeds grew out of its stone walls. There were intermittent cascades, but the canal was otherwise flat, the water stretched like braided glass. There was an occasional bridge. I walked up the canal, then followed the narrow paths between houses. All the doors were open, but I could not see through the screens. I heard voices. Running water and dishes (lunch was over), but I only saw one person: an old man in a doorway wearing baggy pants tucked into

white rubber boots. A large cat with mottled dark fur stretched in a gutter. *Do you remember?* it moaned. *The you inside you?* Golden curtains in the window of the schoolhouse. Gardens covered in green mesh. Bundles of kindling stacked against the burnt-wood houses. I envisioned snow falling in the middle of summer.

The torii gate in front of the shrine was made of old, gray wood. Two lightning-shaped pieces of white paper (shide) hung from a thick, colorless rope. I walked up the stone stairs. I passed beneath the lightning, then turned around and looked out through the gate—the lightning became eyebrows—over the roofs, into the sea. Fifteen islands were visible. The islands were the same. The sea was the same. Where the trees around Oko met the sky was not the same, so the sky was not the same, and maybe the sea and the islands were not the same either. Was the shrine the same? It resembled a shelter, beneath which a well of dark green water was sleeping. *I am here by the well at your house, grandfather. I see a flicker in the dark when I pull water up by the rope.*[2] But I did not see Midori's face in the water, divining the depth of his grandfather's descent into dying. Nor did I see my great-great-grandfather's feet, floating in the shadow of the reflection of his feet floating in an electrified cloud, in the air above Oko. I saw instead my great-grandmother.

*I could imagine his had not been the main branch but an offshoot of the family*
        *A branch family goes out into the world, it splits off*[3]

Midori never mentioned his mother. My father never mentioned his grandmother. No one in my family ever said her name. But her name was there, a snake-like map inside a circle on the wall above my grandparents' bed:

I was told that the snake-like map inside the circle was my great-grandmother's signature. That she had invented it when she was young. It evoked a part of my grandparents' past that was obscure to me. And presided over its continuation in the obscurity of their dreams. But I was not told my great-grandmother's name. As if I was being told, instead, to engage with the snake, get lost in the turns of its maze. Very little of the past was offered. The obscurity of the past resided in not understanding, when I was young, that there was any past. Everyone

---

2. Amarnath Ravva, *American Canyon* (Los Angeles: Kaya Press, 2013).
3. Hiromi Ito, "Eels and Catfish," translated from the Japanese by Jeffrey Angles.

existed, as at the opening of a play, as they were, which made their aging strange and terrifying. An error. A breach. To go backwards, to imagine my grandparents as children, for example, or not yet born—that they had parents, who once were children, or not yet born—was beyond my imagination.

My nameless great-grandmother's signature was as clear as it was incomprehensible. Was it a route she walked, that she wanted, needed, to remember? Maybe it was a map of Oko. If I could learn to read it, travel through it, would I be pronouncing, with my body, her name?

It was only after Midori died that I asked about his parents. The simplest question, who were they? Midori's death, or departure to another place, opened up a pantheon of ancestors. He had to have gone somewhere. The pantheon of ancestors was the most likely place, because it was intuitional. I felt it. Therefore assumed it. The ancestors formed a place in which no single individual could be truly differentiated from the collectivity of the dead. And yet, the first ancestor who introduced herself to me *as an ancestor*, was my great-grandmother. Her name is Kawaki Okamoto.

Kawaki was born in Oko on the first day of February 1883. Her father left his wife for a young woman, about whom the only thing I was told is that she was deaf. *She was an illegitimate child,* June said, about Kawaki, *but her father raised her like his own.* A funny thing to say. But the narrative endured: Kawaki, born out of wedlock to a deaf mistress, embodied an offshoot, a branch family splitting off.

Her father (name unknown) was a contract laborer in Hawaii. He worked on a sugarcane plantation for three years, then in a flower shop in Honolulu, before returning to Hiroshima. One day a man came into the flower shop. The man was looking for flowers to give to the wife of the minister with whom he was staying. The man was from Kumamoto. He

too had been a contract laborer, on a pineapple plantation—where he made $9 a month and shared a thatched-roof shack with five men, one of whom tried to kill himself by drinking a gallon of soy sauce—but left before completing his three-year contract. He escaped. And was living with a white minister and his family. The man's name was Geiichi Shimoda. Okamoto helped Geiichi select the perfect flowers. He thought of his daughter back home and asked Geiichi if he had a wife. He did not. He asked if Geiichi would be interested in marrying his daughter. He showed him a photograph.

In the photograph, Kawaki is standing at the edge of the woods, her back to a body of water, which can be seen over her shoulder, articulated by lines of cloud-like waves. The illuminated limbs of a tree hang over the waves. There is a fog in the woods.

The body of water is not real. It is a painting, a backdrop. For presenting Kawaki, as a picture, to her husband, also unreal. Her gaze is steadfast yet distant, with a little fear at the barely legible edge of unknowing. She is holding a small bag with two fingers. She looks like she is going to drop it, on purpose. It will fall very slowly. Then open, like petals in water.

This was the photograph Okamoto showed to Geiichi. Two men, surrounded by flowers, deliberating over the fate of a young woman standing with her back to a fanciful ocean.

*On the boat we were mostly virgins.*[4] I dreamed, at first, of young women flying over aureoles of light, the edges of their bodies illuminated.

On the passenger list of the steamship from Yokohama to Honolulu, Kawaki's *Calling or Occupation* was listed as: *Wife*.

---

4. Julie Otsuka, *The Buddha in the Attic* (New York: Alfred A. Knopf, 2011).

She, like her unreal husband Geiichi, was a contract labor-er. Picture brides were one of the unintended consequences of the Gentlemen's Agreement of 1907, a political compro-mise between the Japanese government and anti-Japanese white Americans in California. On October 11, 1906, the San Francisco Board of Education called for the segregation of Japanese students in public schools, citing the need to save white children from being *affected by association with pupils of the Mongolian race.*[5] (The Japanese population was relatively young, the number of Japanese students small; Chinese stu-dents were already segregated.) The agreement, coordinated by President Theodore Roosevelt and Secretary of State Elihu Root, appeased both sides of the one-sided war, by agreeing to desegregate San Francisco schools while restricting further im-migration from Japan in the guise of establishing new criteria for the issuance of passports to Japanese laborers. Three classi-fications of laborers were to be permitted: relatives of someone already in the United States; those returning to their homes; and laborers assuming control of land already in possession. Yobiyose Jidai: The Period of Summoning Relatives. Women could become relatives of Japanese men in the United States by marrying them. Proxy weddings (shashin kekkon, picture mar-riages) were performed in Japan. The women were marrying men they had never seen. Except in photographs. They married the photographs first.

The women were given pamphlets by immigration training societies on how to dress and bathe and walk like a western woman, how to sit on a toilet, how to cook food that would not offend their white American neighbors. They were not,

5. Raymond Leslie Buell, "The Development of the Anti-Japanese Ag-itation in the United States," *Political Science Quarterly*, December 1922.

due to legislation dating back more than one hundred years, permitted to become American, but they were expected to behave American. They were expected to be both exemplary and invisible.

The proxy weddings in Japan were not recognized in the United States. When the young women arrived, after three weeks at sea, they were married a second time, in mass ceremonies on the docks. *A young woman is a bride and the groom doesn't always belong to the human species.*[6] The men often looked considerably different from the men in the photographs—older, 10-15 years on average, less attractive; or not the men at all, brothers, friends, cousins. Between 1908 and 1920, over 10,000 Japanese picture brides immigrated to the United States. The unintended consequence of the Gentlemen's Agreement was the first generation of American-born children of Japanese ancestry, the Japanese Americans. The Ladies' Agreement followed in 1921, ending the emigration of picture brides. The last passport issued to a picture bride was dated February 29. It was valid through the first of September.

In the first of Akira Kurosawa's dreams, a young boy stands at the gate of his family's house and stares into the rain.[7] His mother comes up behind him with an umbrella. *You can't go out today*, she says. *The sun is shining, but it is raining. Foxes hold their weddings on days like this. They hate it if anybody watches.*

The boy defies his mother and walks out into the rain. He enters the woods. Trees are tall and feathered. The rain falls in curtains. Out of the mist and rolling fog comes the sound of rattles and drums: a fox wedding procession. There is a bride and a groom and twelve attendants. The bride is wearing the

---

6. Etel Adnan, "Sea."

7. Akira Kurosawa, *Dreams*.

traditional white hood (tsunokakushi, resembling a squid mantle). The procession moves very slowly. The boy watches from behind a tree. The foxes see the boy spying on them. They turn their heads in unison. The boy, seeing them seeing him, runs away.

When he gets home, his mother is standing at the gate. *You saw it, didn't you? You saw something you shouldn't have.* Her voice is lower than before. *An angry fox came looking for you. He left this,* she says, pulling a tanto knife out of her robe. *You are to atone by cutting your belly open. Go quickly and ask for forgiveness. Until they forgive you, I cannot let you back in.*

*But I don't know where their home is,* the boy says.

*Of course you do,* his mother says. *On days like this, there's always a rainbow. Their home is beneath the rainbow.*

She slides the door closed. The boy, gripping the knife, leaves the house in search of the fox's home. He walks into a field of richly colored flowers, mountains rising before him.

It was not the canal or the narrow paths or the lightning hanging from thick colorless rope or the torii or the shrine but everything and nothing at once that evoked my great-grandmother. I felt her sleeves, her arms inside her sleeves. Was there a flag somewhere channeling the ocean in incisive, wave-like snaps? Her sleeves breathed a silken coolness. I felt the nostrils of caves and a sudden decrease in temperature, the exhalation from an old, expired earth. But her arms were warm, a warmth that was, within the silken coolness, euphemistic. Her arms were familiar. I had been inside the sleeves before. There was a memory of a light once having illuminated the sleeves. Not just her arms, her whole being.

How can I explain the embrace of a ghost? Arms open and extended, not even arms. The whole body extended and open. But the embrace, arrested, is unconsummated. The two embracing bodies never touch. An irremediable abandonment burns, like a swallowed polestar, down the spine.

I traveled one hundred years and thousands of miles to connect with a place that may or may not have had anything to share with me about my past. I started with Midori and the feet of his grandfather's corpse. The pilgrimage was to that. But the ghost, in Oko, was me.

I stood with my back to the shrine, looking through the torii gate at the sea, and where I had been feeling at peace, I now felt anxiety. I wanted to get closer to the feeling of my great-grandmother, but I did not know where to go. I chose a narrow path back down the hill and wove my way through its maze.

In the second of Kurosawa's dreams, a young boy, serving crackers to his sister and her friends on Hinamatsuri (Doll's Day), sees a young girl in a light pink robe in the hall of his family's house.[8] The boy asks his sister who the girl is, but his sister insists there is nobody there. He slides the door back. The hall is empty but for a potted spray of peach blossoms. *Have you got a fever?* his sister asks. The boy, agitated, goes into the hall.

At the end of the hall is an open door. Standing in the bamboo outside is the girl in the light pink robe. The moment the boy sees her, the girl turns and runs into the bamboo, accompanied by the sound of a small bell.

He follows the young girl through the bamboo into his family's peach orchard. The orchard is terraced up the side of

---

8. Akira Kurosawa, *Dreams*.

14

a hill of bright green grass, but there are no peach trees, only stumps, and as soon as the boy enters, he is met by a troop of guards. On the terraces above are kings and queens and their retinue of maids and musicians. Fifty-nine figures, the life-sized incarnations of Hinamatsuri.

*Listen carefully*, they say, their voices booming. *We are never going to your house again. Your family cut down all the peach trees in the orchard. We are the spirits of the trees. We are the life of the blossoms.*

The boy starts crying. The dolls laugh, saying that he is only crying because he cannot have any more peaches. The boy, offended and suddenly empowered, scolds them. *I can buy peaches at the store! But where can you buy a whole orchard in bloom?* The dolls, disarmed by the young boy's sensitivity, change their hearts. *Let us allow him to see the peach orchard in bloom one last time.*

They arrange themselves on the terraces and commence a performance of etenraku (music from heaven). The fifty-nine figures spread the colors of their regalia across the orchard. Reed and bamboo flutes and pipes, koto and drum. Peach blossom petals begin to fall. The dolls turn into peach trees. The boy, admiring the music, the colors, then the orchard in bloom, hears the bell again, then sees the girl, and runs after her into the orchard. Once he enters, the trees disappear, replaced by stumps. All the trees but one: a sapling, with peach blossoms.

Midori had dreams of depositing his dead grandfather's feet in the sea, like sending boats to the horizon. He walked down the hill and slipped his empty hands into the saltwater. He had not anticipated being stung with regret — had he accidentally washed off his grandfather's feet? He smelled his hands. They became, for a moment, his grandfather's feet, bars of soap.

He would think of his grandfather's feet again, years later, while waiting to board the *Africa Maru* in Yokohama, alone, en route to Seattle, fish breaking the still surface of the harbor, turning mid-air, disappearing into ovals. The memory of his grandfather's feet, his grandfather a toppled pillar on a white towel, overgrown now, becoming a mound.

In what tradition is the washing of the feet a prerequisite to the journey, on foot, of the dead into the afterlife? Midori's grandfather's footprints would gradually be swept from the house. Would the aura come back? His grandfather's face reared up like a pale pink fish, then evaporated. Midori was left with the image of cotton balls sticking out of his grandfather's nostrils, his ears. He was sealed, could neither hear nor breathe. Midori felt like that too, tried to shake it away.

To say that a village is on the edge of extinction is to say that its future is strictly memorial. That the village's inhabitants are few in number and decreasing, without likelihood or possibility, even, of being succeeded. Maybe it is a diagnosis that makes it easier to colonize a living place with the presumptive and proprietary desires of the imagination.

At the far western edge of the village was a small graveyard, well-kept and proud, surrounded by bushes, overwhelmed by the sound of cicadas. They were loudest in the trees above the graveyard. The village itself might have been a momentary resurrection for the benefit of the nostalgic youth who followed his great-grandmother and her fading, still sonorous bell.

There are, traditionally, two graves: the burial grave and the ritual grave. The burial grave is where the dead are buried. The ritual grave is where the living go to visit the dead. Sometimes these graves are the same. Sometimes not. The ritual grave could be divided: where the dead were born, where the dead died, anywhere, in whatever form, the dead may be perceived and remembered. An altar in the house of the living, a stone in a graveyard, a painting in an alcove, a book.

I live with Kawaki's picture bride photograph; it rests against a large (3-foot-by-5-foot) mirror. The mirror and its reflection, over Kawaki's shoulder, are descendants of the painted body of water behind her, and I worry that the photograph tethers Kawaki to dimensions she would not recognize. She would not recognize my face, coming in and out of focus, attending, so I think, to her memory, which is synonymous with trying to keep it alive.

A grave is anywhere we leave an unrepeatable part of ourselves. A part that has broken away. It provides ritual guidance to the vulnerable, oftentimes humiliating, necessarily mundane act of waiting to die. The grave of what living remains.

The hour was silent. The water held the ghost of a temblor. The boats, moored to the seawall, rocked, making low, gulping sounds. A starfish was stuck to the end of the wall, drying out in the sun. Viscera clung to its mouth. Or asshole. Still wet. There was still life in the star, even though its own life had ended. Like an old, elongated, mysteriously maintained mirror that once hung on the wall of a shrine, maybe a house, above a memorial shelf. A mirror in which smoke from incense, vaguely colored, light purple or green, had imprinted itself as a streak. In which foreheads were always creased, eyes closed, eyebrows drawn to-gether. In which the trees overhanging the stone stairs were reflected more accurately, and more often, than the faces that showed up in the foreground. A star burning into the sea, to live on in the blood of perpetual waves.

The ancestors are always arranging, the hands reaching from all generations to locate me in a body that is also theirs.

We returned to Katsuragahama. It was the weekend of the summer festival. A stage was erected in the pines, facing the sea. Eight young women in spandex, sports bras, and windbreakers were rehearsing a dance to Missy Elliott's "Work It," a coda for the poet's ancient ode to the pines. For the next several hours, boats entered the harbor. The beach filled with people. Umbrellas and tents mushroomed in the five hundred pines. The fireworks started in daylight, filling the gray-blue sky with pale flowers. Jellyfish propelled down through the color spectrum until colors could not go any further. The faces of the five hundred pines flashed. Night rose. The silhouette of the poet, and his passage back into the life he lamented, sparked, then withdrew. The burning ends of each explosion twirled, for a moment, like spirits communicating the order of their future, then turned away from each other, enclosed in their own autonomous orbits, before vanishing into the sea.

## FACES

*Come again in one hundred years*, the woman says. *The colors will be at their peak.*

Flowers are mounted on a wall. The wall is in a small room near the front of a temple. The flowers are pink with white highlights on green, but if it is one hundred years before their colors will be at their peak, how can I be sure? I mourn not knowing, then wonder: will it always be one hundred years?

*By then the camellias will be perfect*, the woman says.

Perfect, I think . . .

Sounds like, *over* . . .

Then says, *They will be most themselves.*

The flowers float on a paper scroll. They seem already old, at least one hundred years. They look like they are sleeping or meditating. Why are we looking at the flowers? We are trying to get into the temple, but the woman has stopped us. What does she want us to see? The temple, the city surrounding the temple, the mountains surrounding the city, one hundred years surrounding the living.

The flowers elucidate the vision, in my mind, of a family: green, conductors of the sun, the ancestors; white, highlights of the sun, inspiration; and pink, the suggestive face, the spectacle of the new generation. But the flowers do not promise anything. It is the woman who is asking us not only to imagine the flowers, but ourselves, our own faces, in one hundred years. My face: pressed through the back of itself, will have evaporated, will be waves.

And it is not the flowers, exactly, but their colors. The colors are alive, still in the process of manifesting themselves. Are they real? Many scores of people face the wall. How much do I love them? *Perfect*: everyone is walking slowly, compelled through the illustrations of the landscape by faces that are, depending on each second, as beautiful and coherent as they are a tragic, unfathomable dough. The colors flash and improve over time, but what about one hundred years after that? Time, light, weather, attention, though the woman does not say what will happen.

At night, the white disappears. Sky, clarified, concentrates a small panic.

When will I be most myself? Will I ever be? Is it only a matter of time?

The woman, meanwhile, stands with strangers in front of the wall and talks about the flowers. She repeats herself over and over. She will not be alive in one hundred years either, so even she, who knows the flowers better than anyone, better even than the soul who painted them, will never really know the flowers. She is a stranger too. I love what the woman is saying and I love looking with her at the flowers on the wall, because I know that I will not be coming again in one hundred years and that one hundred years has already passed.

*Do not simply look at the bewitching lights*, a voice says. *You should also pay attention to the areas of shadow.*

When Midori was nine, he boarded a boat. The boat was long and large, and it loomed, to Midori, like a small, floating city. It was black on the bottom, white and open on top. It had black and gold chimneys. Thick rope grew from the boat to the shore where it was knotted around enormous white anvils. People ascended gangplanks and disappeared into holes. Four hundred thousand people lived in the city facing the small, floating city. Fish rose and turned mid-air, disappearing into ovals on the still surface of the harbor.

Midori arrived with his three older brothers, but only he was to board the boat. Setsuo, Makeo, and Yoshio had failed the health exam. They would have to stay behind. Midori would have to go alone. The small, floating city was not only the passage between the brothers' world and the new world, it was already the new world. Midori and his brothers shared the same body. At home, they were four. In the unknown, they were one. They shared the same health. It was being divided that made them unhealthy.

Many years later, after Midori died, June began writing, in two journals, her recollection of Midori's life. In the journal with the blue cover, she wrote, *The rest of the boys passed their physical in time and joined the family*, while in the journal with the green cover, she wrote, *Because of the expense of staying in Yokohama trying to pass their medical exams, they gave up their dual citizenship and left on the next ship for Seattle.*

Midori's brothers were born in Hawaii. They were American citizens. Midori was conceived in Hawaii but was born in Hiroshima. He was not an American citizen. Between when he was conceived and when he was born, their mother returned, with his brothers, to Japan. He, along with his parents, was a Japanese national, ineligible for citizenship. He became, when he climbed the gangplank and entered the hole, an immigrant. He was the foreigner, and healthy. His brothers were unhealthy, and citizens. The city facing the small, floating city was Yokohama. The boat was leaving for Seattle.

It was the first week of September 1919. The small, floating city floated away. A mountain rose in the sky. It had the appearance of omniscience, of knowing and having known every passage of every era, all fortune and nightmare, including the pitiful saga of Midori. For a brief moment, a white cloud touched the mountain.

The crossing took three weeks. Midori slept underwater. Nothing but water in an immeasurable circle, and it seemed, to Midori, they were heading in no direction at all. For three weeks the world was an island, the horizon a stubborn defense. And yet, the boat met, every morning, the sun rising from it, and every evening, the sun in its wake.

On the boat with Midori were hundreds of young women. They were traveling across the ocean to meet men they did not know. These unknown men were the young women's husbands. The young women knew the men only from photographs. Midori was, like the young women, going to meet a man for the first time. He too knew the man only from photographs. His father's face was remote, yet burned with the energy of a firework, spinning, throwing off light. His father had given him his name, and because his father insisted his fourth child be a girl, he had given him a girl's name: Midori.

*Across the ocean, sparrows looked for camellias to sleep on, but they only found prickly sage.*[9] Shadows, soundless euphoria. A black wave, another ship on the horizon. The young women

9. Don Mee Choi, "Diary of a Translator," *The Morning News Is Exciting* (Notre Dame: Action Books, 2010).

were paragons of what Midori was feeling: a small spasm lost in the reticence between home and the unknown. They were supposed to feel already a part. But home dissolved upon departure. They held their photographs as fragments of a map. Midori was their youngest. They honored his dreams. His dreams simplified the anxiety of their own. And yet, he wanted also to be the men they were going to meet. He wanted to be the relief of a known man.

Surely the young women knew his father, surely their men knew his father, surely all men know each other. Weeds floating out of the horizon prophesied hair on the heads of men. The young women stood as if on a balcony over a performance in the waves. *Transfixed, the attending maids stared at the circles receding from the point where bubbles and foam were thrown up from the sinking bodies, until the last wave died and the bubbles ceased. Then one by one they offered a prayer, climbed the bulwark, and hurled themselves in the waters' depths.*[10]

In 1919, an estimated 267 Japanese picture brides were admitted into the United States through the Port of Seattle. Midori arrived on September 27. Looking into the crowd from the line of passengers filing down the plank, he recognized his father instantly.

Fifteen thousand years ago there was a lake. The lake was 3,000 square miles across, 2,000 feet deep, and contained by a massive ice dam. It is believed to have been the largest ice-dammed lake in the world. For 3,000 years, the dam broke and re-formed and broke, emptying and remaking the lake, carving canyons and rivers hundreds of miles west to the ocean. When the lake was empty, it was a valley. When the lake was remade, the valley floor was

---

10. Helen and William McAlpine, *Japanese Tales and Legends* (London: Oxford University Press, 1958).

a lake bed. When the lake rushed out, the fossils were exposed. When the lake was remade, the fossils were buoyed by the rising water. The fossils rose from the water into the sky and hung in the air over the water, burnished by the sun into misshapen mirrors. When I arrived in the valley, the lake was 15,000 years gone, the sky was yellow, and the valley was filled with smoke.

On the wall of a barracks in a decommissioned military fort in Missoula, Montana, hang three black-and-white photographs of a Japanese man dressed in women's clothing. The man is wearing a light-colored dress, white gloves, small black shoes, and a wig of black curly hair, and he is holding a purse. Two of the photographs show the man with other men, in suits and ties, one in a three-piece suit, one in a hat. The third photograph shows the man sitting in a chair facing into a mirror.

The photographs are surrounded by photographs of Japanese immigrants (Issei) and Japanese American men and women (Nisei) who were, by order of their president, forcibly removed from their homes along the Pacific coast and parts of the U.S.-Mexico border and sent to temporary detention centers, then to concentration camps in remote valleys, high deserts, and swamps, where they were incarcerated for the duration of a war being waged by the country in which they lived and were, in majority number, citizens, on behalf of the freedoms of which they had been stripped. Detention center, concentration camp: basic units of space the United States has devised for the populations it has written into its self-image as refractory, unassimilable, alien.

In the third photograph, an older man adjusts the young man's black wig. A white slip is loose on the young man's body. His feet, in black shoes, are resting on a small shelf below the mirror. He is not looking directly at himself but slightly away.


I saw, one morning, a man made of ash. He was short, not quite five feet, had no features, and was moving very slowly. Moments before, there had been a thunderclap followed by a flash of light. I was in the house where I grew up. I had just woken up. Every light in the house was on.

I was sleeping in what had once been my parents' bedroom. Putting on my glasses, I noticed, first, that the lights were on in the room. The lights were also on in the bathroom, second, then, third, the whole house. Only the hallway was dark, which was when I noticed the man made of ash. He was in the hallway and was reaching the top of the stairs. His body and head and hair were black, a shadow, yet corporeal, with shadow smell, but not burning.

Midori had died a month earlier, in September 1996. I was not there when he died. I did not wash his feet. I did not see his corpse. I was not there when he was cremated. I was not at his funeral. My father and his siblings sat in a nondescript church, surrounded by white women they had never met, and wept. I could not see the man's face but knew it was Midori. I found myself seized by the desire, arising from a terrible feeling that I had abandoned him in his dying, to see him every morning for the rest of my life. He was moving slowly into another room. By the time I had thrown myself into the hall, the man, Midori, was gone.

I followed him into the other room. The room was empty. It was the room I grew up in. The walls were white, with a patch of blue on the largest wall. The room was being painted. Two south-facing windows were warm. Out the window were trees: a row of tulip trees, then gray birch, thousands, interminable. Two slatted closet doors were closed. Furniture had been pushed into the center of the room and covered in white sheets. I went to the closet, slid open the doors. The closet was empty.

I was suspicious of the walls. Someone could slip into any crease, any shadow, and disappear. The patch of light blue took on the dimension of sky. I ran my hands along the sky, feeling for any misgiving, a seam that might open onto a second sky. The sky became the wall of an ancient, limitless monument. Weaker, crazed, I grew angry—at the room, the wall, the sky, the morning light, my inability to read this room in which I spent eighty-eight thousand hours, to recover, in its center, my grandfather. He had chosen to return to my room, so I felt, I feel, I need to preserve the room, my relationship with the room, in its present, uncontaminated form, for whatever might emerge from the wall.

When I called my sister Kelly to tell her that I had seen our grandfather, that he was in the house, she said:

*It was a dream. You were dreaming.*

*But I'm awake*, I said. *I haven't gone back to sleep.*

## THE NIGHT OF THE DAY MY
## GRANDFATHER DIED

The night of the day my grandfather died, I went for a walk in
the woods. I was in my freshman year of college, upstate New
York. Train tracks ran through the woods to Canada. A ditch
ran alongside the tracks. I was walking in the ditch when a
train appeared, moving very slowly. It sounded like it was going
to grind to a halt or fall apart. It was a freight train, but I saw
faces, heard breathing. The walls of the train were constellated
with thousands of eyes and as many haloes of breath, respiring,
through horizontal slits, an emerald light.

The train was interminable. It took the moon traversing
night for it to pass. After it passed, small lights flickered on the
tracks. Reflections of the eyes or sparks off the wheels. Then
people appeared, a procession, carrying lights, swinging them
like censers. I could see their faces in half-illuminated fragments. What I could see was young. I was young too but felt
old and unreal. They did not seem to see me in the ditch. They
did not lift their eyes from the tracks.

After they passed, the woods grew lighter, and I became
aware of where I was standing. The trees arching over the tracks,
the stream in the ditch, the light of dawn in the stream. In the
wake of the train and the procession, the woods seemed static,

silent and still. The grinding of the train gave way to the sound of insects turning down.

The events of that evening into morning became my first image of my grandfather's afterlife. It was the first thing, obscure and overflowing, onto which I projected what I did not yet know was grieving.

## DEATH VALLEY

Midori wanted to return, after death, to the desert. He wanted his ashes scattered in Death Valley. On November 9, 1996, we gathered on a hill on the road to Stovepipe Wells. Midori's ashes traveled, in a clear cellophane bag in a wooden box, by car from Denver, North Carolina, to the airport in Charlotte, by plane to Las Vegas, and by car to Death Valley.

We chose a hill and walked up. I had the feeling we had gathered as strangers, that each of us was walking alone. That with Midori's death we had been particularized by our relationships with him, each of us compelled by what we shared with him, what we did not share with each other. We each found a rock that reminded us of Midori. We built a monument. The monument amounted to a prototypical effigy. The sun was high. June was wearing a white turtleneck and jeans. There was a purple cactus with luminous spines. Midori's ashes were gray, a puzzle cut into one trillion pieces. June scattered his ashes with a spoon. *Scattered* is not the right word. June *dressed* the rocks with Midori's ashes. She *planted* his ashes, while walking in a circle around them. She *released* them.

My aunt Risa read a letter. She sat beside the monument. The letter was addressed directly to Midori. Plaintive, almost pleading. Her voice shook. She was the only person who spoke. She became a child. The nakedness of her becoming a child

amplified our lack of courage, our silence. We might have thought our emotions were bound up in silent observance and not, as they were, petrifying. I felt embarrassed. I thought I was embarrassed by Risa becoming a child, but I was actually embarrassed by my inability to grieve. To speak plainly, uninhibitedly, to Midori. That I was, in the company of my family, my grandfather's ashes, and the magnanimous indifference of the desert, self-conscious. I wanted to join Risa in childhood. But I could not get there. I was even more childish than a child. My childhood had not yet been consummated by the sensation of having been left. I was stunted, with no way yet to move on.

Fifteen years later, November 2011, we returned. On the way to the hill, Kelly and I gave June a camera and told her to take a picture of anything she wanted to remember. Despite being married to a photographer, she rarely, if ever, took pictures, rarely, if ever, touched Midori's cameras. We were standing on the front porch of a jerky shack in Beatty, Nevada. We showed

her how to take a picture. We wanted to see what she was seeing, what she found interesting, in the desert, where Midori
was. Where, she said, she would join him.

She held the camera in her lap. We turned into Death
Valley. We drove toward the dunes. The landscape looked familiar. Its familiarity was an illusion, a ruse. What looked familiar,
to our desert-less eyes, was repetition. We might have thought
we were driving against it. We were being enfolded, were already part of it.

When someone chooses the site of their burial, the place where
they want their ashes to be scattered (*dressed, planted, released*), are
they imagining the relationship that will form between the place
and their family? Within and beyond the desires of the dead, the
living set down the order, the rituals, of death, and follow it, or
not. They are deferential until, unable to bear the desires of the
dead any longer, or forgetting them, or thinking, mistakenly, that
they are not being watched, they become defiant.

Following Midori to the site of his desire was to follow
him nowhere. The desert was the end. Or the opening onto a
new existence, on this side of which we were halted. Not being dead, we did not know that. We were proud, arrogant, yet
stricken, suddenly, with uncertainty.

A memorial exists in the present, must exist and be attended
to and maintained in the present, therefore must constantly be
renewed. In the intervening years, the hill moved. There was
disagreement. Risa and my uncle Sano scrambled up two different hills. (My father was not with us. Did his absence con-
stitute a third, maybe even the most accurate hill?) We walked
June up several hills. She held onto us as if we were leading her
to a baptismal spring. Then we walked her back down. Rested
among the straw-colored brush. Our inability to find the hill,

and the monument, was, to me, consoling. It reinforced not only the privacy of death, but the privacy of memorialization. I did not say that out loud. June was eighty-five. Her feet were killing her. What is the relationship between a woman nearing the end of her life and a pile of rocks in the desert meant to mark the memory of her dead husband?

The phone rang. June was out. Midori answered the phone. *Hello? It's your daughter. Who? Tell Mom I'll be there on Friday. When? Write it down.* The doorbell rang. Midori looked at the phone. The phone was on a small table with a bowl of glass eggs next to a porcelain doll.

Midori pretended he did not know who we were. Kelly and I held the phone to our ears, and he would say, *Nice to meet you,* and we laughed. A better game would have been if he had said, *I know exactly who you are, and I am going to tell you,* in which he would tell us exactly who we were and who we were going to be, even describing where we would die, what we would be wearing, who we would be with, the weather, the hour, the minute, the expression on our faces.

Kelly and I were in the garden. Midori pointed at the mountain across the valley from where he and June lived in El Cajon, California—where they lived before moving to North Carolina—and said: *See that mountain? Close your eyes. Count to fifty. When you reach forty-nine, open your eyes. I will be standing on the top of the mountain, waving at you.* Then he disappeared. We counted to fifty but could not stand it past thirty. Everything on the mountain was Midori. Every shadow, every cloud passing.

Soon, you will not see a mountain. You will not see, on the face of the mountain, the shadow of a gargantuan spider. You will not see the shadow of the gargantuan spider rushing down the face of the mountain.

A wooden eagle hung on the garage wall. The eagle held a stars-and-stripes sash in its talons. The garage had white carpet. *That's how clean the streets are,* June said.

I remember the sun. Glassy, white. I remember a red tomato in the garden. I remember a shirtless man with a rope

over his shoulder, a bee hovering above a pink flower, a tall desert landscape with sandstone buttes, a snake-like map inside a circle, a young woman holding a basket on her head.

Midori's ability to cross the valley and climb the mountain in the distance was possible, permissible, because everything in the desert was, to us, completely new and unknown. We took its magic for granted.


Driving out of Death Valley, we crossed a fox. Low and sleek, it drifted across the road. Our headlights caught its eyes. It paused, turned its head. Its eyes were green. It had the face of an old man. Who had not aged. It continued into the brush, at the pace of a body in total sympathy with its surroundings. I thought of the foxes in Hiroshige's woodblock print, the foxes convening at the base of the enoki trees, arriving in a procession winding deep into the distance—bright, the brightness of full moons cast on rocks on a beach, each fox illuminated by a single flame (kitsunebi, foxfire), each flame an attendant, lighting their way.

Foxes, in Japanese mythology, can turn into humans, in some cases by means of climbing into their bodies. They are often portrayed as tricksters. Sometimes vengeful, especially when their territories or private acts—weddings, in particular—have been trespassed. But they can also be benevolent. It is determined, in large part, by the behavior of humans, how they impose themselves on nature and, posthumously, on each other.


Familiarity inspires affection—a crush, infatuation. What of the affection that is formed by being drawn into relation with a person or place, a landscape, that remains wholly unfamiliar? Midori was watching. To see if we could find him, hoping we would not.

My first published work was a short story about my grandparents. I wrote it my senior year of college. My workshop professor, the novelist Sheila Kohler, encouraged me to submit it for an award. It was fiction but ended up winning for nonfiction. It was called "Lighthouse." In the story, I visit my grandparents on the coast of Oregon (where they never lived). One morning, Midori goes to the beach to take pictures of a lighthouse. He does not return. June and I look for him. We enter the redwoods leading down to the ocean and find him passed out on the path, camera around his neck. We struggle him up the path and back home.

"Lighthouse" was one of several stories I wrote about Midori, all of which had him wandering in the wilderness. My preferred method was to create a landscape in which Midori—an old man, a child—was free to do nothing, was free, like an actor without a script, to improvise. The freedom, however, was mine, imagined, and not entirely without manipulation. I was enthralled, even as I was frightened, by Midori's dementia—the ways he lived in several times and places at once, the ways he withdrew or was withdrawn from us, his personality, his body, his breath, each moment, the ways I imagined the devouring of one's brain might look like from within. That is what and how I wanted to write.

In this story, while Midori recovered in bed, I took his film to be developed. I wanted to see his lighthouses. Every photograph was of my grandmother—*reading a book, standing at the kitchen sink with her back to the camera, sitting at the table with her elbows on a straw place mat and her face in her hands, watering her tomato plants, standing in the driveway with her work gloves . . . pictures of my grandmother in mundane poses, always off-center, haloes of light around her head or her hands, blurred-out backgrounds, foregrounds, lines radiating out from her eyes, her expressions minimal and relaxed, lacking self-consciousness.*

We stayed in a motel in Lone Pine. In the morning we were going to the ruins of Manzanar, the concentration camp where 10,046 Japanese immigrants and Japanese Americans were incarcerated. I thought of Midori's first wife, about whom very little was known, and about whom no one said anything. She was incarcerated in Manzanar. She and Midori had separated not long before, in December 1941. She was named in Midori's FBI file: Margaret Ichino.

June and I shared a room. I asked her questions across the brown carpet. My questions were the same ones I always asked. But the stories she told—which she had told, and which I had heard, many times—were transformed, somehow different. She looked, in bed, with the blankets pulled up to her chin, much younger, a teenager. She told stories, answered my questions, as if she was dreaming. As if the stories were from a life she had not yet lived. Her stories were prophecies, visions.

She listened to Midori's stories for forty years. His stories were acts of burnishing the parts of his experience he wanted to share, to pass on. They were abridged, incomplete. Acts of negation, refusal. His stories included very little, if anything, about Oko or his dead grandfather or Yumi Taguchi, being left by his mother in Nakanose, three weeks on a steamship in the Pacific, meeting his father for the first time, growing up in Seattle, being the only *alien* in a family of citizens, Margaret Ichino, the hatred that forced him out of California, his incarceration in Missoula. His memory began to deteriorate.

After Midori died, June began writing her recollection of Midori's life. Her blue and green journals cover the late 1800s through the late 1960s, with holes between events so enormous they become events greater than the events June remembers. She wrote in cursive. Her letters lean, virtuous, and stubborn, as if into a wind, as if they might fall forward or begin levitating. Then she stopped writing. But now, in Lone Pine, fresh from Death Valley and with the afterimage of the foxfire on the ceiling, the stories were set in motion again. They returned to their purest form, behind and beyond which the experience of June's life with Midori was protected—from the future, my questions. Was peace being made with the fragments? Was she finally alone, free to reorder her memory?

I fell asleep watching the ceiling fan, the blades turning slowly enough for the space between them to inflate a flower of illuminated rays inside its languorous shadow.

The next morning, Kelly and I looked at the pictures June had taken with the camera we gave her. She had only taken one: Kelly and me, standing outside the jerky shack in Beatty, Nevada.

## THE HOUSE THAT NO LONGER EXISTS

At night, the roofs resemble the sea. A cloud passes beneath the moon. The fields between the houses are blue. Trees line the edge of the fields. The roofs are tiled in waves. Clouded moonlight curls in the tiles. The trees are tall and feathered. The fields are low, white aisles between rows of blue. When the cloud passes, blue becomes green. Sleep is illuminated. Another cloud passes. Then everyone is awake.

Small villages support the dead. Then the moon is full again, and everyone is in bed. Small villages seen through breaks in trees overflow uninhabited space onto the road. If the sea, then a sea of tar, thick and rolled into motionlessness: a world waiting in the hiatus of sleep and not meant, while the people sleep, to be seen, except by the moon, ghosts on the road.

One day, Midori came home from school to find a note from his mother on his pillow.

*I've gone to America. Will send for you and your brothers.*

Suddenly the room, the whole house, felt old, unfamiliar. The light from outside formed alienating shapes on the floor, which advanced, very slowly, like the edge of water overflowing. Midori saw his mother standing on a boat, holding a small bag, staring straight ahead, into the first rays of *America*, distant as a planet.

Yumi Taguchi lived in a small house by a green river in Nakanose, Kumamoto. She lived with her son Kumaki (a doctor), his wife (name forgotten), and their two children, son and daughter (names forgotten). Yumi Taguchi's husband, Kimata Shimoda, an alcoholic, was dead. Between the river and the house was a stone wall, with occasional breaks to the water.

One day, Yumi Taguchi's other son Geiichi's family arrived: Geiichi's wife Kawaki and four sons Setsuo, Makeo, Yoshio, and Midori. Geiichi was in Hawaii. Kawaki and the four boys had been living on an island off the coast of Hiroshima, where Kawaki was from, and where Midori was born. After Kawaki's father died, the family moved to Kumamoto. Now there were six young children in the house. Yumi Taguchi had never met her youngest grandson, Midori. He was six, almost seven. Kawaki did not stay long. She returned, alone, to Geiichi, leaving her sons to their education and their grandmother. For two years. *I think this affected Midori's whole life with a little sadness,* June said.

It was not long before the day of their arrival became a distant memory, a rectangle of light at the end of a long, dark hall. Then it was not long after that the day of their departure became a distant memory. And not long after that Nakanose became a distant memory.

Geiichi's brother Kamaki, the doctor, was also, like their father before him, an alcoholic. The morning after he died, his wife shaved off her eyebrows. Yumi Taguchi slid the door back. One hundred years later, the house was gone. The stone wall too. Only the rectangle remained, though out of its frame, in the air, unencumbered.

*Your grandfather's legs were carved of wood,* Yumi Taguchi said, then pressed her hands together and disappeared. Midori wondered, are her legs also carved of wood? *Each leg is the spirit of a person who is no longer with us*, Yumi Taguchi said. Midori thought of his other grandfather, who had died in Hiroshima. His feet. He remembered feeling lost in their lack of smell. Midori envisioned a soap bubble, round and wet. It rolled along the path, through the trees, bounded along the limbs and leaves, and caught the sun, casting a purple cataract on the ground. Wooden legs were hanging from thin, weathered beams. Hundreds of wooden legs—aged, spotted, stained, dark, laced with black characters, though some were pale and new. It seemed, when the legs came together like chimes, that they could become bold, climb up the beams, run away.

How will I remember her face? More and more formless, yet familiar, I can feel it. A small sun in mind, plain yet lost, as though baked into a larger sun, the leaven of an old, fading memory.

When Midori disobeyed Yumi Taguchi (he thought), she sent him outside to pull weeds. He went to the river. A handful of weeds was a knife. Yumi Taguchi made him remove his shirt and lie face down on the floor. He closed his eyes and imagined a family living in the dirt under the house. She bundled the weeds tightly in her hand and lit them. The weeds began to smoke. She waved them above Midori as if she was signing her name on his skin. It was not the burning of the weeds that mattered but what Yumi Taguchi was making permanent. Midori, the dutiful harvester of weeds, smelled the smoke, the impoverished incense of wood, burning hair, crushed grass, Yumi Taguchi's knees. The weeds held the memory of *behind the house.*

My great-great-grandmother Yumi Taguchi's house no longer exists. Or it exists as a letter from a mother to her son, suspended in the air like a window without a wall.

The day I visited where the house no longer exists, there was smoke in the air and the smell of grilled eel. There was a river and, in the middle of rice paddies, a graveyard. The town did not exist either. Nakanose became Kashima, Namazu to the west, Kaminakama to the east, mountains to the south, a river flowing west into Shimabara Bay, the Ariake Sea.

We traveled by bus. We departed from a parking lot in Osaka, ten at night. No station, but a small park across the street from a parking lot, folding tables, young people with clipboards. We sat on a curb beneath a young tree. On the bus, seats were assigned by last name. A piece of paper taped to the front seat read: シモダ. I had never seen Shimoda in katakana. I read and understood my name, for the first time, as western, American. Everyone had already taken off their shoes, put on paper slippers, and fallen asleep.

The road was black as a river with no moon. We sailed soundless as fish. Trees tall and feathered. No reading, no lights, no one snored. We were sailing off the map, the map dissolving in our wake. I was feeling foolish and sentimental. I tried to write a poem. I scratched a few lines while looking out the window. The thick, feathery trees started to wake up.

In the beginning, I was blind. I fell asleep, and when I awoke the country was blue. We were crossing the Kanmon Strait. Seven hundred years before, the eight-year-old emperor of the Heike, facing defeat by the swords and arrows of the Genji, leapt with his grandmother into the waves. Dawn. The shadow of the bus began to float upon the opening to the Inland Sea.

The woman selling tickets in the Kumamoto bus station had never heard of Nakanose. She gave us a map but did not know where on the map Nakanose was. Yoshie, the young mother we stayed with, had never heard of Nakanose. Nor had her father, who lived a few streets over and had grown up there.

They looked at the map and found a post office in a village called Kumamotonakanose—only a few miles from Yoshie's house—but could not tell from the map how to get there.

*All Shimodas are from Nagasaki,* Yoshie said.

Her father drove us around the neighborhood farms in his sedan. The roads were only as wide as the car. We drove past rice paddies and empty greenhouses. It was late July. Most everything had been harvested. There were tomatoes and watermelon. It was hot and overcast. I looked up the names of vegetables in a simple dictionary.

Dear Hiromi Ito,

I am a poet. My partner Lisa (also a poet) and I are going to be visiting Kumamoto this summer—where my grandfather was raised, where my great-grandfather and great-great-grandmother are from—

*Dear Brandon Shimoda,*

*Kumamoto in July, August is awful weather! Just hot, hot, hot, hot and humid, humid, humid! But I am going back there probably July as well.*

*So how can I help you?*

I am wondering if you might have any suggestions of places to visit—museums, small restaurants, temples. We are very simple travelers—content to sit, look at trees, walk, eat, talk with people.

*I've never gotten these mails before, asking me advice about Kumamoto sightseeing from unknown people who know me by my books. So I am little bit puzzled how to react.*

[pause]
*We have 800 year-old camphor tree, and it is gorgeous.*

*I go to the riverbank as I weep, and there the water flows steadily along,*
*I don't know how deep it is, I look and see myself reflected once, twice*
*upon the water, there I am, if I had a regular life I could live to be more*
*than a hundred years old, but can I make it that far?*[11]

The poet Hiromi Ito and her daughter Zana met us at the
bus station. *I never turn right*, is the first thing she said, out the
window of her car. She drove us, by way of a series of left,
ever-tightening turns, to a small noodle shop where we ate
sea eel tempura with soba off round wicker plates with potato
cream and ginger, and drank tea from the buckwheat foam
strained from the pot. I told Hiromi that we were looking for
my dead grandfather and for a town called Nakanose. She had
never heard of it. She called her friend Baba-san. Baba-san
was the first person we met in Kumamoto who had heard
of Nakanose, but we never actually met Baba-san, fitting for
a guide who knew of a town that no longer existed. Hiromi
offered to take us.

I do not remember the way. We passed through a landscape made nondescript (I remember MOS Burger) by the
anxiety of trying to remember instead of seeing everything we
were passing.

We crossed a bridge. Hiromi pulled to the side of the road.
*Nakanose,* she said. A demolished wall. Smoke in the air and the
smell of grilled eel. There was a road parallel to the main road,
and a smaller road connecting them to a levee between the
river and rice paddies. A silhouette moved in a garden near a
small pickup truck. Kase River, but the map said Midorikawa:
Midori River, green river.

In the middle of the rice paddies was a small graveyard.

---

11. Hiromi Ito, *I Am Anjuhimeko*, translated by Jeffrey Angles (Kalama-
zoo, Mich: Sagaing Press, 2005).

Two dozen gravestones. White mold. Black rectangles. A small white house with a gray-shingled roof. Four bushes and a tree. Dead flowers between stones.

Hiromi turned left onto a narrow levee and stopped beside the graveyard. Tiny frogs flamed across the muddy water and sky.

Tiny peaches grew in clusters on the leaves of rice—pink, twenty-five or thirty to a cluster. The peaches were the eggs of the apple snail. The snail lived in the water, emerged to run its eggs up the leaves, where they would be safe.

We crossed the narrow strip of land into the graveyard. There were large bouquets of flowers. Candles melted into small round stones had not yet burned all the way down.

The stones were inscribed with names, birth and death dates. Hiromi spotted a tall stone, with a roof flared like a hat broken by a strong wind, and shouted, *Shimoda!* Three bouquets of pink and white flowers encircled the stone. In front of the stone were a thin white candle and an incense holder stuck to a ceramic plate. The incense holder was a sawed-off pipe. The wick of the candle was black and stuck up like a thick hair. To the right of the candle was a larger incense holder, also a sawed-off pipe, cemented into a white bowl. To the left was a blue ceramic teacup. A can of beer looked refreshing.

Obscured by the shadow of the broken hat:

下
田

Surrounded by pussy willow and plastic flowers, facing west, was the Shimoda family stone. Takayuki Shimoda, an army sergeant in Wolrd War II, fought in Russia, died on the battlefield. He was in his early twenties. *We should give some* thought to the fact that as some names are being recognized, other countless, nameless souls of the same family are left only buried deep in the bottom of the grave.[12] Where were the doctor's bottles? Where were the widow's eyebrows? Where was the shrine of wooden legs?

*Please excuse me, I have to write*, Hiromi said, stepping out of the graveyard.

*But looking at the wide-open landscape around the rice paddies*
*I could imagine how stubborn society must be*
*I could imagine his had not been the main branch but an*
    *offshoot of the family*
*A branch family goes out into the world, it splits off*
*And the descendant of that family*
*In this case becomes a nine year-old boy*
*Crosses the Pacific, goes from Yokohama to Oita, then arrives in*
    *Kumamoto*
*All alone*
*And stands face to face*
*With the grave where generations of the Shimoda family are*
    *buried*
*Next to that[13]*

I ascended the steps to the stone. I ran my fingers over 下田. The graveyard was where people came to worship, but the people were elsewhere. Candles, incense, tea and beer, it had not been long since they had been there. But the graves were coming to ruin. Colors eaten by the sun.

12. Yanagita, Kunio, *About Our Ancestors: The Japanese Family System*, translated from the Japanese by Fanny Hagin Mayer and Yasuyo Ishiwara (New York: Greenwood Press, 1988).
13. Hiromi Ito, "Eels and Catfish," translated from the Japanese by Jeffrey Angles.

I felt, standing in the graveyard in the middle of the town that no longer existed, a strange kind of peril. I felt as close as I have ever felt, before or since, to acknowledging the ritual of my own decomposing body being visited by strangers.

What family was I feeling? There was no sense of a face staring down from the clouds. But a quiet cancellation. I was inside no nation. I was concentrating. But even my concentration was undone by the mediumship of the grave.

As we left the graveyard, two gray herons flew in front of Hiromi's car and landed on the water. From behind the levee, a third heron rose, then landed apart from the other two. Then a fourth and a fifth appeared low in the sky and joined the other three upon the water. Then Hiromi turned right, which she swore she would never do, out of the rice paddies. The last rice paddy we passed was planted with hundreds of black flags. The wind was passing through their solemn demonstration. Frogs continued to spring, the flags' shadows growing larger, five gray herons hanging suspended.

## THE CAMPHOR TREE

A monk killed himself beneath a camphor tree. He was young, had grown up not far away. He knew the tree as a child. There was never a time when he did not know the tree. Becoming a young man, the monk became a monk, and, as part of his duties, took care of the tree. The tree was eight hundred years old. It possessed the attentiveness of a mother—non-judging, with light filtering through its leaves, casting whole, unconditional refuge.

What did it mean to take care of the tree? Sweeping the roots, delousing the leaves, stabilizing the wooden crutches beneath branches growing near to the ground, even though the tree was already balanced. Which meant being there: watering the cups, walking in circles. The tree takes care of me, thought the monk. That was part of his care, not a matter of one outlasting the other.

The monk sat beside the tree's enormous trunk in a square of dirt and raised a cup of poison to his lips. The first sip released the clarity of eight hundred years—neither sacrifice nor calculation nor witness to the execution, but the stripping of inherences leaving a form of sainthood in the guise of each visitation.

We drove through hills of dark green orange trees. When we arrived, two young boys were flying kites. A man in light blue and yellow was trimming the grass around two young trees with scissors.

I walked around the tree. I looked into it, through it. I was self-conscious, felt absent-minded. At first, my absent-mindedness was intentional. I wanted to absent my mind. The tree, with its trunk thick as the foundation of a house and limbs three humans wide, reflected and possessed the entirety of the world. The order of things was complete. It overwhelmed beauty. It was composed of too many aspects to be one. Or, rather, its beauty was transgressive, but its transgression was humble. My absent-mindedness became a liability. It took the form of wanting to remember.

The tree's agelessness cast a light upon my humanness. I was human, that was my age. Everything the tree had seen, experienced, endured, was there before me, revealed, while I, human, was the obscurity.

The accumulations of the world led not to judgment but silence. The monk became part of what he loved. He knew his love would outlast him. Poisoning himself beneath the tree would give him the advantage of ascending up the tree. The tree would drink him. The poison he drank became part of the earth. I could see it hovering like a statement struggling to form.

Poison is only half of itself. The other half is the heart—the heart that is suggestible.

Zana found the wing of a tamamushi beetle beneath the tree. The wing was iridescent. The colors changed in Zana's hand. A shape-shifting eyelid plucked from the face of a sleeping giant. The tamamushi was gone. What it had shed, what it lost, was not only what gave it flight, but beauty. That is a human supposition. The tamamushi bore a hole into the wood where there was no light, and fell asleep. The wing, disembodied, continued to iridesce. It did not need the body, only light. I felt my own gravity prohibiting the light from realizing a special aspect of itself. The tamamushi's body was indistinguishable from the grass and weeds and dirt. It was the wing that gave it not only its charm, but flight. Would the tamamushi be even more charming now, without any of its resources, small and sky-less and simple?

In the long drawn history of the island, the tree is small. Only if eight hundred years could be reconstituted in the present moment would the virtue of its smallness be revealed as the virtue beyond years—the tree's wide-reaching limbs, the millions of leaves pivoting imperceptibly with the sun, radical Atlantis below.

The countryside was dark with orange trees. The oranges were radiant in the dark aggregation, yet seemed to be hanging from nothing. I could not smell them, and I wondered how it was that they never lost their color.

# THE WOMAN IN THE WELL

A woman was thrown down a well for refusing the advances of a man. The woman, Okiku, was young, but the man, whose name was any name, was any age. He fixed his gaze on the woman. The woman resisted. The man was, to the woman, a dark fragment of roiling, low-lying space. The woman was, to the man, uncooled porcelain, perfectible. His gaze passed through the woman to the core of his own disintegration, the facet of his own narcissism over which he had the least control: a facet that perverted every hopeful aspiration into hatred. The man saw in all the bodies that passed before him in servitude the fetching scions of his own body.

The man was a wealthy samurai. His holdings included a remote country estate. The woman was one of his servants. She lived in a small room, with a view of a tree, its old, ingenuous elbow. The samurai wanted the woman to be his and thought that, because the woman was working for him, she already was. The man made his desires for the woman explicit. When the woman resisted, the man retaliated. It was not a decision but a reflex. For him, love was inseparable from punishment.

The man had a set of ten heirloom plates. White, each painted with a scene from his ancestral village. The plates had been passed down hundreds of years. He loved the plates because he loved being, in his mind, the culmination of those hundreds of years and the bearer of the memory of his ancestral village. He spoke of the plates as if they had been forged of the teeth and bones of each family member who touched them, beginning with the first, nameless, forever faceless family member, who preceded counting, a perennial firestorm in a cloud.

One of the woman's tasks was to take care of the plates: polish and keep them protected in a lacquered wooden box and display them when called for. She was the only one permitted to touch or even look at the plates, outside the narrow space of ceremony. She permitted herself moments of sympathy. The man observed this. He observed the bond that was forming between the woman and his plates. He became disturbed by the back of the woman's head, tilted down, as if she was memorizing, whispering into, the plates. It was clear the woman was establishing a more intimate relationship with the plates than he could ever awaken. He became disturbed by the woman's hands on his plates. He became disturbed by the woman's fingers stroking his ancestral village.

One day he accused the woman of losing one of the plates. She swore she did not lose it but, fearing punishment, vowed to find the missing plate for him. Except it was not missing; the man had hidden it. The woman counted the nine remaining plates so many times that she began to believe nine and ten had switched places.

The man watched the woman grow shadows and curl into herself with self-doubt. He knelt down beside her and, feigning sympathy, told her to forget about it, forget about the tenth plate, it is gone, there is nothing more to be done. Then he said, I will excuse you, that is, if you agree, at last, to be my lover. The woman, recognizing the trap, refused. Nine was nine.

Ten was the consummation of bondage. The man, rejected, became enraged. He picked up the woman, carried her to the edge of the woods, and threw her into the well.

The first time I saw Okiku she was hanging on the wall of a small izakaya in Izumisano, Japan. I was eating pickles and chicken at the bar when I turned around and saw, on the wall, an androgynous, stone-like wraith with long hair rising, like a vapor, out of a well.

In 1830, Katsushika Hokusai painted Okiku. He gave her the long face of a night flower, light blue and white, with solemn eyes and white eyebrows. Her long ears are shells in her long black hair, which cascades down the body of a snake. Her lips are closed over the small hole of her mouth like she is sipping night.

Was Okiku's murder a cautionary tale or a mandate for an eternity of murders? She appeared nightly at the mouth of the well. People could hear a voice counting to nine. Then, in the absence of ten, a scream. The scream flashed through the fog, stood roots on their ends. Okiku's murder transitioned from an aural hallucination into a ghost story. It was neutralized by the fantasies of the living, fantasies derived from the boredom born of privileged security masquerading as fear.

Do you believe in ghosts? The answer, whether Yes or No or I do not know, is Yes, because I believe in the human desire to be afraid while simultaneously overcharged with disbelief. Fear manifests the ghost and its opposite: the ghost of the ghost, coming closer. How often is it asked, for example, if a ghost believes in the living?

Before he reentered his house, the man flicked a pumpkin leaf from his ankle. When he had picked the woman up to carry her to the edge of the woods, his view was momentarily obscured by her robe. He tried to blow the robe out of his eyes. But his vision was already consumed by what he was attempting to forget, replicated indefinitely, the most he could hope for in his life: becoming a dog, emaciated, always hungry.

The man had, years earlier, visited his ancestral village. It was small and surrounded by tall, leafless trees, at the edge of a city that seemed perpetually enclosed in fog. It took several days to get there, and, once he got there, he wanted to leave. He was overcome with a feeling of dread, which rose from the ground, up through the soles of his feet.

When he returned to his estate, images of his ancestral village began to visit him. Every time an image came to mind—a bloodless white house in the shade of an impassive chestnut tree; dozens of thin leafless trees all the same height; chocolate roof tiles; horse chestnuts; gray faces peering through hard windows—he thrust it away and immediately resorted to justifications in the form of both romantic and childish returns to his plates. Except that the plates and the man did not have any rapport. He had trouble touching them. He stopped at the box.

Hokusai gets up, leaves the room, leaves Okiku, goes into another room, goes to sleep. *If only Heaven would give me another ten years,* Hokusai says, *I could become a real painter.*

Tsukioka Yoshitoshi (1839-1892) also painted Okiku but as a much different woman. There is no snake body. Okiku's face is not a disfigured moon. Death has been beautified. In his painting, Okiku's hair hangs over her eyes. Her hands are raised, as if to hide her face or the reflection of her mourning, but her hands are lost in her scarlet sleeves; her feet too are lost in the folds of her robe. She wears a blue-and-white robe over her scarlet robe. Her sash is green, drawn tight with a tiny pink bow.

Yoshitoshi did not paint Okiku as a ghost but as an angel.

She appears, in the branches of a dark tree, as a singing revelation of the well, which contains, by an inversion compelled by her spirit, the heavens. The opening of the well can be seen through Okiku's robes. She mourns beyond prayer, beyond resurrection. Her form of revelation is a nearly forgotten tributary.

For Yoshitoshi, Okiku's beauty was essential. For Hokusai, what was essential was Okiku's transformation, her death as the consequence of having possessed threatening knowledge.

Okiku lives below the brushes of the painters. She lives below the reflections of the faces of people who peer into the well in order to punctuate, with their curiosity, the story they have heard, in order to hear it again, in the counting of plates. She holds each plate like a framed photograph. She looks at each painted scene as if it was her own mother, her father, her grandparents, alone or together, on a hill, in a distance she feels first in her throat. She touches braided glass, bundles of kindling, colorless rope, five or six stones, bushes, a starfish, the glaze that appears and disappears across the face of each plate, and she remembers.

The heavens? Okiku's scream draws a cloud over her mother, her father, her grandparents, over her great- and great-great- and great-great-great grandparents, as real to Okiku as she is to them, who feel a momentary darkening and look up from the mundane hour in which they are standing to see the sun slip behind a cloud. Okiku's scream is minted above the opening of every well. If the counting is suspended at nine, if the tenth is never counted, the world is populated by many billions of tenths, each immortalizing a moment of recognition.

## GREAT GRANDMOTHERS

*In what market-place of the universe are the bargains made that have traded my need for my great-grandmother's?*[14]

For a moment it seemed the Japanese women in my family were waging a campaign against living in the United States. My great-grandmothers, both young, twenty years younger than their husbands, immigrated to the United States as picture brides, had children, then returned with their children to Japan. June's mother, Asano Yamashita, took June with her from Utah back to Fukuoka. Midori's mother, Kawaki, took her three sons with her from Hawaii back to Hiroshima, where her fourth child, Midori, was born.

In the United States my great-grandmothers' history was cast as an unfathomable spring of perversity and suspicion. Their humanity was a matter of national opinion, contingent upon the reckoning of strangers who knew or cared little about Japanese history, except where it intersected with their own lives in the present, in what they violently believed was their rightful homeland. Asano and Kawaki were not eligible for citizenship in the United States. They could not become

---

14. Joy Kogawa, *Obasan* (Boston: David R. Godine, 1981).

"American." And yet, their qualifications for being or becoming American were constantly on trial.

When Asano and Kawaki returned to Japan, their husbands (my great-grandfathers, Masakichi and Geiichi) stayed behind. When Asano and Kawaki, on the other side of the ocean, pictured the United States, the faces of their husbands materialized, rippling, pond-like. Asano and Kawaki were summoned over the ocean twice, the second time with the advantage, or disadvantage, of knowing what to expect. They were summoned to deliver to their husbands a family, which their husbands needed to consummate their determination toward permanence. American-born children were the advent of legitimacy.

My grandmother, June Shimoda, was born Chizuko Yamashita on a farm in Utah, July 17, 1926. *She left my father*, June said of her mother, Asano. *She took me with her back to Japan. We were in Japan for a few years. We eventually came back due to family pressures. She felt I needed a father. Maybe my father demanded it.* They boarded the *Siberia Maru* on August 2, 1929. On the ship's passenger list, Asano's *Calling or Occupation* was listed, like Kawaki's, as: *Wife*.

The first thing I heard about Asano was that Masakichi threw her against a wall. I pictured her body sliding down a wall onto the floor. On a camping trip with another couple, Masakichi chased Asano through the woods with a knife and raped her. Asano did not tell her daughters until many years later. Susie and June carried their mother's rape with them into old age. It became a matter of fact—they told me at the dinner table, between other stories—and the keystone to their mother's miserable life. *The coldest place I've ever been*, Susie said, about the graveyard in rural Utah where Masakichi is buried.

When Masakichi was fifteen he emigrated from Fukuoka (town unknown) to the United States as a contract laborer for a railroad company. His first wife, also a picture bride, *contracted the flu and passed away*, according to June. Asano was sixteen when a marriage was arranged with an unknown man in the United States. They shared the same family name, although, June assured, they were not related. Masakichi returned to Fukuoka to bring Asano back to the United States. They settled in Utah.

What was the land like? *Flat.*

Nothing but flat? *Nothing but flat.*

*The Wasatch Mountains were in the background*, June said. *From Ogden you could see the mountains. But from Ogden down to our farm was flat. When she saw the farm where she was going to live . . . needless to say, it was a shock. She was a sixteen-year-old girl, the baby of the family, with ten older siblings, babied all her life and now's she marrying this man twenty years older than her, with an eight-year-old son, and she has to be the boy's mother?*

*Her first child—my older brother Jay—died when he was young*, June said. *He drowned in a pond. I was a baby. He must have been old enough to walk, as he walked right into the water.* June called it a pond, but Saburo, her brother, called it an irrigation ditch. One was a carat of white sun, the other an unremarkable fold in the earth. *We farmed dirt*, June said. The ditch was either not very important or absolutely essential to the farming.

I asked Saburo about Jay's death. We sat next to each other at the Sea Empress Chinese restaurant in Gardena, California, on the occasion of a Yamashita family reunion. Saburo and I had not seen each other in many years. Everyone claimed we looked like each other. Jay died before Saburo was born. *The same thing happened to me*, he said. He described going down to the irrigation ditch with his siblings—June, Teddy, Susie—for a picnic. *We had peanut butter sandwiches and saltines. At some point everyone looked around and saw there was someone missing.* Saburo could not swim. *I almost died, but June jumped in and saved me. She reached around in the water until she touched my head and pulled me out.* The way he described it made it sound like he was saved by touch alone.

I knew at an early age that June did not swim, that she refused to even enter water. She took Kelly and me to Lake Norman, but sat thirty feet back from the water's edge. This was before I learned about Jay. I did not know, until he told me, that Saburo was also claimed by the ditch, or almost, and that it was June who saved him. There was something of the irrigation ditch in Saburo's eyes. His eyeballs bulged, like they were floating in water, like he had opened his eyes underwater and stared directly into what had seduced his dead brother.

I met Asano once, at the Keiro Nursing Home in Los Angeles. She was wheeled down a long, dark hall to where my sister and I were waiting. I was very young and did not, until the moment we were placed in front of each other, know she existed. She rose before my sister and me like a mountain. She was gowned in white, a precipitous snow-covered slope. She sat in a wheelchair. Her mouth was a black hole without teeth, lips sucked in, rushing backwards through her face. She looked, in the dark, ammoniac hall, like she had been plucked from the sanctuary of her world and abandoned before two preposterous children and their plundering, idiotic gazes. Her face was lunar, beyond grieving. I was young, beneath understanding. And afraid. I was looking into the illegible expression of oldest age.

## PEOPLE OF THE FIRST YEAR

For two generations, the Yamashita and Shimoda families crisscrossed the Pacific on steamships, Yokohama to Honolulu, Honolulu to Yokohama, Yokohama to Seattle, San Francisco to Yokohama, the *Africa Maru*, the *Kaga Maru*, the *Tenyo Maru*, the *Siberia Maru*, 1885, 1896, 1909, 1919, 1924, 1929. Masakichi was fifteen the first time he crossed the Pacific from Japan to the United States, thirty-six his second. Asano was sixteen her first time, twenty-two her second. June was one her first time, three her second. Kawaki was sixteen her first time, thirty-four her second. Geiichi was twenty his first time, thirty-three his second.

Geiichi was among the second wave of Japanese contract laborers to arrive in Hawaii. The first wave arrived in 1868. They were recruited off the streets of Tokyo and Yokohama by an American businessman named Eugene Van Reed, who convinced the Japanese government to issue passports. The voyage was expensive. Hawaii agreed to pay one-fifth, and Van Reed would pay the rest. Shortly before the ship set sail, the Japanese government collapsed. The new government did not honor the agreement, so Van Reed, with his undocumented immigrants, disappeared into the Pacific. Gannen Mono: People of the First Year.

For six years, between 1870 and 1884, the Japanese government prohibited emigration to Hawaii. Hawaii's plantation owners pleaded with Japan to end the prohibition. The need for Japanese contract labor in Hawaii was a consequence of the whites' decimation of the indigenous population and the Chinese Exclusion Act of 1882 banning immigration from China.

The second wave of immigrant laborers sailed from Yokohama aboard the *City of Tokio* on January 20, 1885. *They were in a terrible financial situation,* June wrote, *so when Geiichi found out the Hawaiian pineapple plantations were looking for workers, he volunteered.* They arrived in Honolulu on February 8, the first group of government-sponsored contract laborers. They were from Yamaguchi, Hiroshima, Kanagawa. The *Tokio* was followed later that year by the *Yamashiro Maru*, which carried over nine hundred Japanese—men and a small number of women and children—from Hiroshima, Kumamoto, Fukuoka. The foreign ministry advised what to bring: three sets of ordinary clothes, a short-sleeved kimono, tight-fitting pants, summer nightwear, bedding, mosquito nets. *The Yamashiro Maru* arrived June 17, 1885. The *Yamashiro* was followed by the *Peking Maru* (1886) and the *Miike Maru* (1893). Between 1885 and 1894—the Government Contract Period—over 29,000 contract laborers traveled on twenty-six voyages from Japan to Hawaii.

In 1893, the U.S. government backed a coup, led by a small cadre of white businessmen, to overthrow Queen Lili'uokalani and the Kingdom of Hawaii. Hawaii became a territory of the United States five years later, in 1898. *The danger that Hawaii might be orientalized was greater than in the days of unstinted Chinese immigration. In fact the fear that the islands would be annexed by Japan was one of the prime factors in the demand for annexation to the United States.*[15] Two years later, it gained an elected government under the Hawaiian Organic Act of 1900. By 1905, nearly 10,000 contract laborers had left Hawaii for the mainland. By 1907, that number had quadrupled. White landowners and laborers on the mainland, especially in California, believed themselves to be under siege and broadcast their hysteria to state legislators. Racism and xenophobia were translated as concerns over labor conditions. Theodore Roosevelt called upon the secretary of commerce and labor, Oscar Straus, and the Bureau of Immigration and Naturalization, to enforce Executive Order 589 subtitled, *An Act to regulate the immigration of aliens into the United States*. Straus was born in Germany, immigrated as a child to the United States, and was America's first Jewish cabinet secretary. He was particularly devoted to ridding

---

15. Katharine Coman, *The History of Contract Labor in the Hawaiian Islands* (New York: Macmillan, 1903).

the country of *anarchists and criminals*, among whom he included *aliens*. EO 589 ended the movement of Japanese laborers and their families from Hawaii to the United States.

Midori was nine the first time he crossed the Pacific in 1919. The *Africa Maru* sailed from East Asia to the west coast of the United States and South America. It was built by the Mitsubishi Shipbuilding Company in Nagasaki in 1918 and replaced the *Hawaii Maru* on the route to and from Seattle. Its maiden voyage began on March 28, 1918. It sailed from Yokohama and arrived in Seattle on April 11. It weighed 9,476 tons.

Mitsubishi's shipbuilding operations were among the largest in Japan. It had three shipyards near downtown Nagasaki and employed, by 1945, over 36,000 people, 7 percent of the city's population. In addition to the shipyards, Mitsubishi owned, in Nagasaki alone, an arms company—manufacturing, among other munitions, submarine torpedoes—an electric company, a power plant, and steelworks.

The *Africa Maru* was being used as an army passenger-cargo ship on Tuesday, October 20, 1942, when it was torpedoed off the coast of Taiwan by the USS *Finback*, a submarine under the command of J. L. Hull. The *Yamafuji Maru* was also hit. The *Finback* was performing poorly that Tuesday; it missed thirteen out of twenty targets. The *Africa Maru* sank to the bottom of the ocean.

## THE FIRST JAPANESE TO BE
## PHOTOGRAPHED

Hikozo Hamada (1837–1897) was the first Japanese to become a citizen of the United States. He was thirteen when he and his stepfather boarded the *Eiriki Maru* sailing from Edo to western Honshu, via the Inland Sea. The *Eiriki Maru* sailed into a storm, was shipwrecked, and drifted for fifty days across the Pacific. Seventeen men, including Hamada, survived. An American ship rescued the men, brought them to San Francisco (1851).

Manjiro Nakahama (1827–1898) was fourteen when he and four friends wrecked their fishing boat and became stranded on Torishima, south of the Izu Peninsula. An American whaler rescued Nakahama and his friends and sailed them beyond the horizon, first to Honolulu, then to the mainland United States (1841). Nakahama eventually made his way to Massachusetts.

Oguri Jukichi (1785–1853) was twenty-eight when his freighter, the *Tokujo Maru*, sailed into a storm off the Izu Peninsula and drifted for sixteen months across the Pacific. Three men, including Jukichi, survived. A British ship rescued the three men off the coast of California. They eventually sailed north past Alaska to Russia back home through Hokkaido.

Tsunenaga Hasekura (1571–1622) was forty-two when his ship, the *Date Maru*, sailed from Japan to the coast of California, reaching Mendocino, before sailing south to Mexico (1613-1614).

Otokichi (1818-1867) was fifteen when the *Hojun Maru* sailed into a storm. The ship was carrying porcelain, rice wine, and one thousand bags of rice. The rudder tore off. The mast blew down. The ship drifted for fourteen months across the Pacific, eventually reaching the Olympic Peninsula of Washington (1833). Three men, including Otokichi, survived.

Sentaro (1830s-1874) was a cook on the *Eiriki Maru*, and was among the men, with Hamada, brought into San Francisco in 1851. A photographer from Baltimore, Harvey Marks, made daguerreotypes of the shipwreck's seventeen survivors. Sentaro sat first. He wore a striped yukata and had his hair done up in a topknot. He placed his hands on his lap, looked at the man, then the box, then into its oddly sentient glass.

Sentaro appears, in the photograph, very far away, more distant even than the brief, inconceivable moment in which he was *taken*. Not only his face continues to translate across the distance, but his hands. They rest, fingers straight, on his thighs. Displayed, as if Sentaro is preparing. To turn them over, reveal what they are holding.

Hands captured—enshrined, as in a photograph—evoke, or emit, one's mother in her youth. Sentaro's mother's hands emerged, for a moment, in San Francisco. Came forward, in search of relief in the solemn victory of her son being seen. Her hands are proprietary, protective. Maybe all photographs belong to *mother*, are occasions for *mother* to express her eternally en-ergized dreams.

When Sentaro's mother was young, what did she imagine of her life? What did Sentaro add to her imagination? It has been written that Sentaro was the first Japanese to be photo-graphed. But who was in control of the representation? Did Sentaro ever see his daguerreotype? His double led a distinct life, which may or may not have communicated, in any way, with Sentaro's original self.

He joined Commodore Perry's expedition to coerce Japan into ending two centuries of seclusion. He sailed with Perry aboard his flagship, the *Powhatan*, named after the indigenous people of eastern Virginia who had been largely eradicated by white settlers and the spread of infectious diseases in the mid-1600s. *Powhatan* was a fitting premonition for the United States' form of diplomatic action in Japan. Sentaro's crewmates called him Sam Patch. He became the first Japanese Baptist in the late 1850s. He eventually returned to Japan, where he died of beriberi. He is buried at Hodenji Temple in Tokyo.

Otokichi changed his name to John Matthew Ottoson and became a British citizen in the 1840s. He returned to Japan twice—the first time disguised as a Chinese man, the second time using his British last name. He is buried in a Japanese graveyard in Singapore.

Hasekura was baptized Felipe Francisco Hasekura in Madrid in 1615. He returned to Japan in 1620. His grave is believed to be in one of three locations: on the edge of Osato in Miyagi; in a temple in Enfukuji, also in Miyagi; and at Komyoji Temple in Zaimokuza, Kamakura.

The location of Oguri Jukichi's grave is unknown.

Manjiro Nakahama, aka John Mung, returned to Japan in 1851. His grave, in Tokyo, was destroyed during World War II.

Hikozo Hamada was baptized "Joseph" in 1854 in Baltimore and became a U.S. citizen in 1858. His grave is in the foreigners' section of Aoyama Cemetery in Tokyo.

## THE CHARACTERS

A five-page pamphlet titled *Photographers Using Non-silver Processes*, published by the Center for Creative Photography (CCP) at the University of Arizona, Tucson (2002), lists 140 photographers, including Imogen Cunningham, Tina Modotti, August Sander, Edward Steichen, Alfred Stieglitz, and Edward Weston. The 111th is Midori Shimoda. Next to his name is a question mark.

I had just moved to Tucson, was living five blocks from the CCP. I was thinking about Midori and thought, in a moment of missing him, that I would look him up online. The pamphlet appeared. With his name and the question mark. The question mark spoke to me. It seemed to be mine, my question. I called the CCP. I explained to the woman on the phone that I had come across a reference to Midori; did they have any information about him? It seemed a long shot. Moving to Tucson had nothing to do with Midori. I did not anticipate there being a trace. The woman (the archivist) was procedural. She asked for my email, then hung up.

*Attached is the cataloging record for the photograph by Midori Shimoda. A Japanese photographer that was in residence a few years ago suggested that Midori Shimoda was probably an alias for*

| | |
|---|---|
| Paul Outerbridge, Jr. | Carbro color (1) |
| Diana Parrish | cyanotype (1) |
| Kathryn Paul | cyanotype (1) |
| Irving Penn | platinum/palladium (2) |
| Michael Peven | cyanotype (1) |
| ? Phelps | platinum (?) (1) |
| Bernard Plossu | Fresson (4) |
| Linda Fry Poverman | vandyke, with Prismacolor (4) |
| Jane Reece | platinum (1) |
| Charles B. Reynolds | platinum (1) |
| Ted Rice | platinum (3) |
| Joyce Robinson | cyanotype (1) |
| Cady Robles-Gates | gum bichromate over cyanotype (1) |
| John P. Roche | carbro color (7) |
| Meridel Rubenstein | palladium (2) |
| Drahomir Joseph Ruzicka | bromoil? (1) |
| Robert J. Sagerman | palladium (1) |
| August Sander | gum bichromate (1) |
| Naomi Savage | gum bichromate (1) |
| John P. Schaefer | platinum (2) |
| J. Keith Schreiber | palladium (9) |
| Klaus Schnitzer | platinum (2) |
| George H. Seeley | platinum (1) |
| | gum platinum (1) |
| George H. Seeley (attrib.) | platinum (1) |
| Midori Shimoda (?) | bromoil transfer (1) |
| Ann Simmons-Myers | gum bichromate (1) |
| Clara E. Sipprell | platinum? (1) |
| Harry Smith | palladium (2) |
| Keith Smith | cyanotype (2) |
| Laurie Snyder | cyanotype (1) |
| Edward Steichen | carbro color? (2) |
| | palladium and ferroprussiate? (1) |
| Alfred Stieglitz | Satista (palladium/gelatin silver) (1) |
| Paul Strand | platinum (23) |

*William Mortensen. The photograph came in the William Mortensen Archive and looks very similar to his photographs. Can you verify that the photograph is actually by your grandfather?*

Yes, this photograph is by my grandfather, Midori Shimoda. He apprenticed with William Mortensen at WM's Laguna Beach, CA studio, in the mid-to-late 1930s. The photo is of my grandfather's sister, Setsuko. Many of his photos from the time owe an evident debt to Mortensen. Is this photo at the CCP?

*This is good news—I can correct the cataloging records for the photograph. If a photograph is cataloged, then it is in our fine print collection of photographs. Your grandfather's photograph is here. If you want to see the photograph, then you need to make an appointment with me. The Study Center is open Monday-Friday, 10am-4pm, by appointment only.*

*P.S. Would it be possible to give me birth and death dates for your grandfather?*

I would love to come in on Thursday morning, 10 am.

Here is additional information on my grandfather:

Full name: Midori Arthur Shimoda
Born: March 26, 1910, Hiroshima, Japan
Died: September 13, 1996, Newton, North Carolina
He was an active photographer from 1933–1973. Apprenticed with William Mortensen (Laguna Beach). Colleagues with Toyo Miyatake.

*We can show you the photograph on Thursday at 10am. When you arrive, go to the 2nd floor and wait in the lobby.*


I was ushered by the archivist's assistant to a long table in a room with no windows. The assistant handed me a box of small, white gloves. When I put them on, I felt like a cartoon mouse, a detective, a serial killer, then a child, and as if I was going to be handling something instructive but ultimately useless, like a fossil. The assistant handed me a box of small pencils. The pencil kept slipping out of my gloved fingers. The feeling of violating the privacy of death intensified. But surely Setsuko would have wanted out of this place. I was visiting her to resurrect from the windowless room the intervention of a presence,

a semblance even, so I could feel, surrounded by the unending desert, and the spirits, living and dead: there is family. *In this glum desert, suddenly a specific photograph reaches me; it animates me, and I animate it.*[16]

In the summer, Midori and his brothers picked strawberries on the Kitsap Peninsula, Washington, on a twenty-acre farm owned by a Japanese American family. Setsuko, at home with their parents in Seattle, dreamed of the strawberry fields. She missed her brothers, longed for them to return, to tell her what it was like, but not everything. She wanted to know only enough to flesh out the image she was creating.

Even though they were alive when I was born, and even though they lived into old age, I did not know—because I was not introduced to—my great-uncles Setsuo, Makeo, Yoshio, and Kikuo (born in Seattle), and my great-aunt Setsuko. They were a secret, or I was. The only sibling about whom I heard anything—Makeo—was incarcerated in Heart Mountain, the concentration camp in Wyoming where 10,767 Japanese immigrants and Japanese Americans were incarcerated during World War II, as if his existence was validated, in the negative, by the government record. Makeo changed his name to Roy. Yoshio became Jack. Setsuo, the oldest, became George. Kikuo, the youngest, also became George. Only Setsuko and Midori kept their Japanese names.

Setsuko was born May 1920 in Seattle, and died one year after Midori, in 1997. While she was consigned to a drawer in the windowless room in the desert, another Setsuko lived on a wall in my grandparents' house. She was one of the inhabitants

16. Roland Barthes, *Camera Lucida,* translated from the French by Richard Howard (New York: Hill and Wang, 1980).

of a museum devoted to the time before I was born. An era, momentous, providential, to which I felt pitifully belated. A shirtless man with a rope over his shoulder, a bee hovering above a pink flower, a desert landscape with sandstone buttes, a snake-like map inside a circle, a young woman holding a basket on her head, connected by threads of light crisscrossing the room, the whole house. It was through these threads, vibrating below the level of (my) perception, that the museum's inhabitants communicated with each other. My grandparents' house was a universe where the past transcended death, transcended the behaviors of the living. If I stand in the right place, I thought, I might be lifted off the carpet and drawn into the wall.

I am curious about something you mentioned in an email back in November, that *a Japanese photographer that was in residence here a few years ago, suggested that Midori Shimoda was probably an alias for William Mortensen.* I am wondering if you remember who that Japanese photographer was, and the nature/context of the conversation in which he made this suggestion.

*The remark that I made is cataloging information that I have since changed. The cataloger at the time, spoke to our photographer in residence. She may have misunderstood him. At any rate, the information is not accurate and not pertinent to your inquiry.*

Midori was enrolled in a photography class at the Art Center School in Los Angeles when he learned about the Pictorialists, including William Mortensen. Mortensen worked in Hollywood before opening a photography school in Laguna Beach, where he inculcated his students with the belief that a photograph could possess the qualities of drawing and painting, a belief that was anathema to an increasing number of purist photographers. Ansel Adams, for example, referred to Mortensen as *the Antichrist.*

Did that mean Adams was Christ? Between October 1943 and July 1944, Adams visited the Manzanar concentration camp four times. His photographs, compiled into *Born Free and Equal,* focus on the aspects of incarceration that sublimate the injustice of incarceration, foregrounding, instead, the spirit of the Japanese Americans, which Adams asserted was *strengthened* by the *acrid splendor of the desert.*[17] His interest was in recording the ways Japanese Americans made use of *conditions beyond their control* and against the backdrop of the *grandeur, beauty, and quietness of the mountains.*

*He told his subjects to smile,* wrote the photographer Brad Shirakawa, in an essay on Adams, adding: *They didn't refuse.*[18] Smiles became weapons in establishing what Adams felt were

17. Ansel Adams, *Born Free and Equal: Photographs of the Loyal Japanese Americans at Manzanar Relocation Center* (Washington, D.C.: Echolight, 1984).
18. Brad Shirikawa, "Looking Back on Ansel Adams' Photographs of Japanese American Internment," *SFGate,* December 6, 2016.

the virtues that most effectively highlighted the injustice. *It is photographs of Japanese American incarceration that naturalize the state of exception with the false assurance of a smile.*[19] Smiles were used to assuage white anxiety, by affirming a kind of loyalty in which white Americans could believe. It was a brutal kind of loyalty, dependent on the Japanese Americans being obedient to the war manifest on all sides, while putting on the appearance of enjoying their own sacrifice.

In a letter to critic Nancy Newhall, Adams reinforced the importance of allowing *no opportunity for anyone to accuse us of any production detrimental to the war effort. Hence, the distinction between the loyal and dis-loyal elements must be made crystal-clear.*[20] The subtitle of *Born Free and Equal* is *Photographs of the Loyal Japanese Americans at Manzanar Relocation Center.* The struggle of the Japanese Americans—if a struggle could be gleaned from the photographs—was the transformative process of assimilation, of becoming American, under the watch, and restrictions, of white America.

Midori looked up the address of Mortensen's school in Laguna Beach, 1737 Coast Boulevard South, and took a bus there from Pasadena. He knocked on the door. Mortensen answered. Midori said he wanted to apprentice with him. Mortensen looked at the Japanese man, and said, *I cannot pay you.* He agreed, instead, to let Midori live in his basement, which was furnished with only a bed frame, no mattress.

The photograph of Setsuko is featured in a book by Mortensen—*Monsters & Madonnas: photographic methods*—and

---

19. Jasmine Alinder, *Moving Images: Photography and the Japanese American Incarceration* (Urbana: University of Illinois Press, 2011).

20. Ansel Adams, *Letters: 1916–1984* (Boston: Little Brown, 2001).

is credited to *Midori Shinioba.* The caption reads: *Part of a series of photographic illustrations inspired by the works of Omar Khayyam, this bromoil captures the truly spiritual happiness of the people of the Orient.*[21] I think of Midori in Mortensen's basement, staring, from the bed frame, up through the ceiling. It seemed especially perplexing that it was a Japanese photographer who had not only questioned another Japanese photographer's ethnicity—the evidence being what he must have determined was an inauthentic representation—but that he had also assumed him, by association and default, to be a white man. Is it possible Mortensen vampirized the personae of his apprentice and his apprentice's sister to effect his fantasy of a *truly spiritual,* and "Oriental," *happiness? The suggestion of traditional Oriental dress,* the caption continues, was *achieved with costume elements of tested photographic effectiveness; the pseudo-Japanese calligraphy successfully balances the composition.*[22] Is it possible Midori vampirized Mortensen's vampirization of him? Midori signed 下田 in the top left corner of the photograph. He inscribed three lines of Japanese text over Setsuko's shoulder. Is it by the presumptive suggestion of *pseudo-Japanese calligraphy* that the text looks like a string of え and す and る and ろ dripped into a song, invocation? And where is Setsuko in the characters?

21. William Mortensen, *Monsters & Madonnas: photographic methods* (San Francisco: Camera Craft, 1936).
22. Ibid.

## DAIMONJI

On a night in August every year, fires are lit on the faces of five mountains surrounding the city of Kyoto. Each fire burns in a shape. The first fire, 大, burns on Daimonji, followed by 妙法 on Nishiyama, a boat on Funayama, 大 again on Hidaridaimonji, and a torii gate on Mount Mandara. The living, in the valley, read the fires as the end of the annual observance of Obon. The dead, whose vantage is more omniscient, without fixity, read the fires as the way to go home.

On the night of August 16, 1988, my family and I walked, with thousands of people, along the Kamo River. When we turned onto a bridge, the thousands of people congealed into an impenetrable wall. Every time one person escaped, a hole opened for a moment before the remaining thousands shifted to close it. If one person fell, they would not fall but stay standing. If everyone fell, they would bend like tall grass. I was ten years old and small. I could see as far as stomachs and arms and shoulders, not the fires on the mountains. If I closed my eyes, I could see the river beneath us, white birds or bowls or paper carnations or cold starfish on the water. The river moved in tribute to the mountains. I closed my eyes and held on to my family. The fires slid into the river.

Years later, Lisa and I walked up the mountain of the first fire, Daimonji. It was late afternoon, July. The sun was starting to go down. The mountain was thick and dark. Occasionally the trees broke and we could see the mountainside, precipitous and watchful as the face of the moon. Hundreds of cement pedestals were arranged in an enormous 大. The roaring, from when I was ten, had not died, but was held in a monumental silence. Stacks of wood covered in white cloth waited in the trees.

Cities, seen from above—from a mountain, for example—evoke the afterlife of ancient, evaporated seas. Kyoto was flat and white and silent but for its circulatory system. There were mountains on the far side of the city, and, in the city, archipelagos of scattered green. We had arrived the night before and spent the day walking the east side of the city. The garden at Heian Shrine was closed, but we were allowed to enter. Nothing was in bloom. Men in sky-blue uniforms and white helmets were in the bushes with shears and rakes and ladders. Japanese tourists, older men and women, stood on a bridge over the pond, throwing baguettes to the ducks.

An old woman crouched on a sidewalk over six small, flat, round fish. She was wearing baggy pants, light gray, and a blue shirt, oversized and frayed at the neck. The six fish were in a small circle of sun. Three were lifeless, the others thinly convulsing. The woman lifted each fish with a pair of flat wooden tongs, turned and then set each fish down, as if over a flame. She touched each fish with the ends of the tongs in a reassuring manner, calming each heart, putting each fish to sleep. Ducks floated past in the reservoir of a small hydroelectric dam, their heads in their wings. A crow, beak open, hopped along the sidewalk. Depending on the time of day, the circle of sun on the sidewalk always moving, the woman moved, and, moving with her, the fish.

I stared into the 大 where a fire would soon burn and felt a tremendous heat. The flames rushing up the precipitous slope, the embers, the heat rising off the mountain, did not veil but clarified the view, and in each cell of fire I could see not the spirits of the dead but the devotions of the living.

The more the living speak and breathe, I thought, the more light and heat are given to the dead. All but wandering ghosts want to be dead, to formulate within the consciousness of their death the continuation of life. But that is life in death, not life. Light and heat are recourses we insist upon to keep life afloat, but that is memory where there is no life. We cannot stop speaking about the dead, breathing up and down their bodies, with which we stock our silences, while fantasizing the contours of the dead as they once were in life, or might have been, but do we ever actually think of the dead as dead?

This is not a description of a wall. Unless the wall, seen from the earth in front of it, standing in front of it, facing it, is the façade of an airless and terminal monument, without openings or rooms, without corpse or opening or room for a corpse, that bends the people who must endure it to worship what they think is buried on the other side. The swarm is stunned. There is nothing on the other side. There is no other side.

We thought to take a different route back down the mountain. We measured our steps carefully down the 大 and entered the trees. We could see the white cloth and Kyoto. Then the white cloth was suddenly extinguished, and we could no longer make each other out. What we thought was a path was where water carved a rivulet, ending in rocks, tree roots and limbs. We had no light. We turned back up the mountain. We groped our way toward the face. It shone through the trees like an ocean. The moon and ocean were the semi-consciousness of the fire.

We emerged onto the face, even more precipitous in the dark. Gravity became fanciful.

Two young men were sitting at the top of the face. We explained to them that we were lost. We knew where we were—at the top of the 大, the city below—but we had no light; going back down would be long and dangerous in the dark. The young men got up and, with the light from their phones, walked with us back down the mountain. We descended gingerly through their bounding pools of digital light. They were studying to be scientists. They had climbed the mountain to watch the sun go down. They were on their way to a festival on a bridge.

When I was young I wore a blue T-shirt that said, I ♥ KYOTO. I wore it every day in the summer until someone asked me if Kyoto was my girlfriend. The same person who said I looked like both Short Round (the Chinese sidekick) from *Indiana Jones and the Temple of Doom* and Major Toht (the Gestapo agent) from *Indiana Jones and the Raiders of the Lost Ark*. Embarrassed, I hid the shirt in the back of my closet. When I was ten, standing on the bridge, I thought: I am going to die. I am going to be crushed into these people. I am small, and, because I am small, I will be trampled. My body is going to slide off this bridge and float down this river, become indistinguishable from the white life, the agents of celebration, the residue.

## DREAMS

My father and I are in Manhattan. We are trying to get to Kelly and Neil's apartment in Brooklyn, but we do not know where the subway is. We stop in at a flower shop. *Cross the bridge*, the florist says, *then turn left*.

There are thousands of people on the bridge. The bridge is dark, without lights. The thousands of people have formed a mass and are moving with tremendous speed, like a river, bodies down a river. *It's a protest*, I say. We try to join, but it is moving too fast, so we wait for the mass to go by. After it passes, we climb onto the bridge and walk across it into the dark.

On the other end of the bridge is a forest of thin trees bearing enormous red fruit.

Neil and I are in a very rundown bookstore. The bookstore consists of four rickety shelves holding mass-market paperbacks. One shelf is taken up with a series of paperbacks, all the same color and size, each with the name of a state on the spine: Alabama, Alaska, Arizona, Arkansas . . . I flip through a few: historical fiction, all by the same author. The author photo shows a young white man with blond hair wearing a military uniform.

Among the states is, oddly, Japan.

The bookstore clerk tells us the author lives down the road, we should visit. We knock on his door. He is not a young man anymore but old, bald, and bloated. His body shakes. He invites us into his office, then disappears. On his desk is a rare edition of the book on Japan. Instead of being a mass-market paperback, however, the book is a series of drawings on a delicate scroll, tightly wound and set into the shell of a living snail. I extract the scroll from the shell and begin unraveling it but unravel it too far. I cannot get it back into the shell! The snail, inside the shell, is like a very wide, very wet tongue and is trying to either push the scroll out of the way or devour it.

Children are waving long glow sticks. It is the anniversary of the bombing of Hiroshima. There is going to be a reenactment. At 9:30 (it should be 8:15), a fake bomb will be dropped. It is called a *spectacle bomb*. Everyone says it is going to be blinding. You can look, but everyone is advised not to. I separate from the crowd—there is a stifling amusement park atmosphere—and stand on a hill to take notes. I discover strange sores and welts on my body, especially my arms, as though my body is reacting to the radiation, though the spectacle bomb is fake and has not yet been dropped. I rejoin the crowd to look for something to eat: soda, potato chips. School buses pull up. Children pile out of the buses. It is 9:00.

Twenty-four years after immigrating to the United States from Japan, Midori returns, via boat, to Yokohama. Upon arrival he is given a gun. *What am I supposed to do with this?* he asks. *Kill the enemy*, he is told. *But who is the enemy?* he asks. *Focus*, he is told. *You are not in America anymore, Midori. You are in Japan.* He stares at the gun in his hands, then looks up. He is alone. It is winter. Snow mutes the smell of smoke.

## NAGASAKI

An old woman pushed a small cart through a park in Nagasaki. The top of the cart was a glass box. Stacks of sugar cones leaned against the glass. The woman leaned the cart back on its legs, spooned rosewater ice cream out of the metal chest into a sugar cone.

There was an enormous tree. A streetcar pulsed and then there were bells. The woman lay down beneath the tree and draped a small towel over her eyes.

At 11:01 and 43 seconds on the morning of August 9, 1945, a U.S. B-29 bomber dropped a plutonium bomb on the city of Nagasaki on the southwestern island of Kyushu. The bomb, named Fat Man, exploded 1,539 feet above Urakami, the Catholic district on the north end of the city, incinerating, in less than a second, 73,000 people.

Mayumi's grandmother was working in a bank downtown. A bottle of red ink exploded on her desk. Customers and co-workers thought the red ink was blood. When she returned to her apartment, she found her cleaning woman, who had been preparing lunch when the bomb exploded. To shield against the flash, the cleaning woman grabbed a frying pan. Mayumi's grandmother found her in the kitchen, dead, with her arm raised, still holding the frying pan.

Cities selected as possible atomic bomb targets at the first meeting of the target committee, April 27, 1945: Tokyo Bay, Kawasaki, Yokohama, Nagoya, Osaka, Kobe, Kyoto, Hiroshima, Kure, Yahata, Kokura, Shimonoseki, Yamaguchi, Kumamoto, Fukuoka, Nagasaki, and Sasebo. May 10, the committee narrows the list to Kokura, Hiroshima, Kyoto, and Yokohama. At the third meeting, on May 28, Kokura and Yokohama are removed from the list; Niigita is added. Secretary of War Henry Stimson, who visited Kyoto with his wife Mabel on their honeymoon (1926), removes Kyoto from the list. On July 24, Nagasaki is put back on the list.

A short distance from where the old woman was napping stands a black pillar on a flattened mound of grass. Around the mound radiate concentric circles in grass, brick, and stone. In front of the pillar are two rectangular stones, black, one larger than the other, the larger resembling a coffin, the smaller a prayer bench. The atomic bomb exploded directly above the pillar. The pillar is glossy. If you get close enough you can see yourself in it.

    A girl with blond hair was walking around the pillar, holding ice cream in a sugar cone. She was with her father. Neither spoke. A shallow creek, ten feet wide, with ivy-covered stone banks and stone paths, ran along the edge of the park. On one of the stone paths, the skin of a snake.

Up the street is the Peace Park. The park is crowded with monuments offered by nations around the world. Weatherworn, they needed cleaning. Women, children, women holding children, children holding hands, hands holding birds, bells, figures contorted in dance, dancers. From Poland, Holland, Italy, China, Germany, Bulgaria, Brazil, Czechoslovakia, Turkey, Argentina, New Zealand, the Soviet Union. The first came from Nagasaki's sister city of Porto, in Portugal. It was dedicated thirty-three years after the bombing, in 1978: Relief of Friendship. Monument of People's Friendship, Protection of Our Future, Monument of Peace, Statue of Peace, Maiden of Peace, Cloak of Peace, Sun Crane of Peace, Triumph of Peace over War, Flower of Love and Peace, Joy of Life, Hymn to Life, A Call, Infinity. Only Argentina included the word War. There is no monument from Great Britain. Seven human figures, naked and stretching, holding each other's hands and feet to form a sphere called Constellation Earth is from St. Paul, Minnesota. Otherwise, there is no monument from the United States.

Late July. High school students stood on aluminum bleachers getting their class picture taken. The boys wore loosely tucked, white button-down short-sleeve shirts with black pants and sneakers. The girls wore dark blue dresses over white button-down short-sleeve shirts, their hair just to their shoulders or shorter or in ponytails. The boys' hair was short. Their teacher wore a dark blue straw hat with a wraparound brim, a white short-sleeve shirt, and a dark blue skirt with tights.

Behind them, half sitting, half standing, was a giant. The giant was shirtless and green. His right arm was raised, his index finger pointing to the sky. Do not take your eyes off the sky, he cautioned. The sky was where the atomic bomb was conceived, from where it fell. Like weather or an act of God.

Seibou Kitamura, the giant's sculptor, was born in Nagasaki in 1884 and lived to the age of 102. *Kitamura's proposal ran counter to the convention of the proliferation of Japanese postwar memorial monuments to peace, love, and hope, which always depicted goddesses*, wrote Tomoe Otsuki, in an essay on the politics of the dismantling and reconstruction of the ruins.[23]

The giant is crude and seems to have been rushed into existence. He does not have a neck. While his right index finger points to the sky, his left arm is outstretched, horizontal. He is not pointing. His fingers are spread. Is he conspiring subliminally with some form of insidious energy? His right leg is folded beneath him. His left leg is propped up. He has long hair. A piece of cloth is draped over his left bicep, hangs over his left upper thigh. His eyes are closed. Is he uncomfortable? His face is wide and withdrawn, frozen. Is he asleep? His smile is not meditative but vacuous. Is he dreaming? His muscles are tight over his ribs. His nipples are Olympic. His hollowness is pornographic.

*Much of the motivation for Kitamura's piece was the product of his pride, ego, and professional ambition*, Otsuki wrote. *During the war, he produced some statues of famous military figures, all of which were muscled, warlike, and immense . . . When* [he] *saw his statue in Peace Park, he stated*, I have become immortal.[24]

The giant does not make me think of the victims of the atomic bomb, living and dead, or the bomb, nor do I see the giant as an injunction to remember the victims, the bomb, to never forget. Instead I see the stale indication that what is being remembered is the injunction itself: remember to remember. The giant's pose, meaninglessly balletic, says that we are much safer at the threshold of memory, just outside of it, where all of our feelings are correct, with no particular object by which to clarify, to be made specific, to be made genuine, real.

23. Tomoe Otsuki, "Reconstruction of 'Christian City Nagasaki' in Postwar Years."
24. Ibid.

Children chased each other through the Atomic Bomb Museum. Some of the children, as they passed a photograph or melted object, made sounds of shock, but they were running so quickly that, by the time the sounds left their mouths, what shocked them had passed, and only the sound remained.

Mrs. Yamashita was on a television monitor on a wall deep inside the museum. I heard her voice before I saw her face. She spoke about the delirium she felt while wrapped—shocked, shaking—in a mosquito net. She lifted her index finger to signal for help, and her finger became infected. Now she was an old woman, speaking to strangers she could not see.

There is the perceived consolation that Mrs. Yamashita is not alone. That she is recognized as belonging to the community of hibakusha, survivors. Belonging that has been, continues to be, complicated, often impossible. Rejection, isolation, shame, silence. Regeneration begins, almost by accident, as sound, wind through the hall of a museum. Mrs. Yamashita can neither see nor hear the other hibakusha. Neither can they see or hear her.

Every night, Mrs. Yamashita's monitor is turned off. Her voice and face are extinguished, mid-sentence. Every morning, she is turned on again. She does not begin mid-sentence, where she left off, but from the beginning. That is a form of suffering the memorial enacts: it will not let Mrs. Yamashita die. In aiming to rescue Mrs. Yamashita from the ashes of Nagasaki, the museum has made her permanent. But she has been divided. Dead outside the museum, alive inside, she has become two people, each separated from the other. I grieve for the Mrs. Yamashita who died. I also grieve for the Mrs. Yamashita who could not be present for her death. The museum invited her to talk. She obliged and was, in one sense, relieved.

The museum ends in a hallway opening onto an atrium in which are displayed on moveable walls chronologies and bar charts and drawings made by children all over the world in one unified yet nonspecific appeal for peace, but by the time anyone reaches this display, they are worn out, sated, ready to return to their lives.

The Peace Museum and the War Museum are the same museum. They outline the lives of wars, ogle the effects of war by displaying those objects—wristwatches, eyeglasses, shoes—that exhibit the power of each war's weapon. To look at a glass bottle twisted and shrunken and to see in it the neck and upper torso of a dead animal is not to consider the life of the bottle or where it was the moment before it was blasted, on which table or shelf it sat, or who held it, what it was filled with, but to look at the weapon that twisted and shrank it and marvel over that weapon's power, that made an animal from an inanimate object.

## THE BATHHOUSE

Mayumi took us to a bathhouse on a hill overlooking Nagasaki. It was a large, lodge-like wooden building. A sign on the front door said, *No Tattoos.* I asked Mayumi if I would be allowed in, and she said, *It's okay, you're a foreigner.* I have four tattoos: my father's (Shimoda) family crest, my mother's (McAlister) family badge, Kawaki's snake-like map inside a circle, and a bride with a hood covering her head.

Men and women separated. I ascended a stairway and entered the locker room, undressed, then entered a large, open bath. Forty, fifty men, middle-aged to old, soaked in tiled baths before an enormous window looking onto a terrace of smaller, individual baths, a rock garden, ferns, the northern neighborhoods of Nagasaki. Men with small white towels around their necks, draped over their heads, men sitting on brightly-colored plastic stools shaving, scrubbing, showering with long-hosed showerheads before mirrors set low to the floor. In a smaller room, men sat on wooden risers watching television. There was an enormous wooden cask of white salt. I was the only American, the only westerner. I wondered if my body was glaring. My lungs constricted. I was holding a white towel the size of a washcloth.

Outside, a long, rectangular bath, covered by a wooden

arbor, set into a landscaping of rocks and ferns, faced Nagasaki. The men's asses were round, folded, double-folded, dimpled, tucked under, tan, saffron, intimations of blue. Old men rose from the bath, water snaking down their leg hair. Men rested on white plastic lounge chairs, wooden benches. No one spoke. Everyone was staring into Nagasaki. The stimulus of naked old men on a ledge overhanging Nagasaki brought together fragments of a recurring dream: ice cream, an enormous tree, a black pillar, a giant, the asses of old men. I rose from the small tub and joined the men in the long, landscaped bath.

I saw the green giant. He was small in the distance, though I could see his right arm in the sky. His outstretched left hand pointed to a willowy dome of trees where the bomb was dropped. Standing at his feet, the poverty of his image had been obvious. From the bathhouse on the hill, the giant was forceful yet even more insignificant. Where were the humans? It bothered me that a giant was needed to impress history upon the people, for the giant was mute, immobile, not human, and was, with his finger raised to the sky, the brainstem of the bomb. I could not help but feel that all memorials for the dead, memorials for peace, were memorials for the bomb.

I was naked on a white plastic lounge chair on the terrace of the bathhouse, looking at a young tree in an enormous pot. The tree was thin, and I was watching clouds pass. A young man, fully clothed, emerged onto the terrace. He approached me directly and said, *You have to leave the bathhouse.* He pointed to my tattoos. I tried to explain that my friend said it was okay, but my friend, Mayumi, was on the other side of the bathhouse. The attendant went back inside, came out again and said, *Yes, you have to leave.* Yes, my body was glaring. I walked across the wet tiles of the bath, aware of my ass withdrawing into the steam.

In the locker room, the young attendant approached again and asked where my friends were. *They're women*, I said, *they're not in here. You better hide*, he said—my arms, he meant—and then left.

## DOMANJU

The first time I visited Domanju, I was ten. I remember a river, black blue and green. I remember a large bell, hanging inside of what looked like the cap of the earth's largest mushroom. I remember a statue shaped like a squid. I remember, on top of the squid, another statue, a young girl, holding above her head, as if in offering to the sky, an enormous crane. I remember, on the sidewalk above the river, a young girl and boy, not statues, ribbons of every color unraveling from their arms, gathering in colorful piles on the ground.

I later learned the young girl on top of the squid had been killed. Her name was Sadako. Sadako was not yet two when an atomic bomb was dropped on Hiroshima. She lived with her family one mile north of the hypocenter. Her house burned down. Black rain fell on Misasa Bridge. Ten years later, mysterious lumps appeared on her neck, purple spots on her legs. Neither she nor her parents thought it was anything serious, but her doctor, whom they consulted to be sure, told her, *You have one year to live*. She moved into the Hiroshima Red Cross hospital.

It is said, by some, that if you fold one thousand paper cranes, you will be rewarded with a long, healthy life. It is said, by others, that you will be granted one wish. Sadako folded one thousand cranes. Some said she folded six hundred and

*94*

forty-four. Maybe she saw a crane rising off the very same river, black blue green water, and perceived some form of salvation in the crane being doubled, flying above and below itself. It flew low over the water, at first, almost touching. Though it flew exactly as fast as itself, its reflection, against the slow current, made it look, underwater, even faster. Then it rose into the mountains.

The atomic bombing of hundreds of thousands of Japanese civilians was translated—sublimated—into the suffering of a solitary and youthful figure. The translation provided the perspective outsiders needed to feel satisfied in their comprehension of both the magnitude and meaning of death. For the living, there was room to be heartened. Other patients in the hospital, classmates, people all over the world, began folding paper cranes. They could, in the act of transforming pieces of paper into consciousness—contemplative, capable of soaring—become the dying girl, as well as the governor of a peace the dying girl did not live to experience. For Sadako, the responsibility was—and continues to be (there is no peace)—a burden beyond all proportion.

Sadako was one of my guides into the atomic bombings of Hiroshima and Nagasaki. The first, though, was another child, Keiji Nakazama. I first encountered August 6, 1945—from the flash of the morning sun off the wings of the B-29, to the ribbons of flesh hanging off the arms of the half-dead—through Keiji's comic book, *I Saw It* (1972). Keiji was six when the atomic bomb was dropped on Hiroshima. Like Sadako, he also lived one mile from the hypocenter. He was about to enter the front gate of his school when a B-29 bomber appeared in the sky, followed by a colossal flash of light. Then the world went dark. A moment later, Keiji came to. He was lying in rubble. The wall of the school had collapsed, shielding him from the blast. Among the first things he remembered seeing were a woman with burned hair and black skin lying in the street; women in underwear, glass sticking out of their bodies; people whose skin had turned blue; people whose skin had turned black; people crawling across roads, looking for water; people lying motionless along the sides of the roads; skin hanging off people's bodies in strips; eyeballs dangling from eye sockets. Keiji's father, brother, and one of his sisters, died instantly. His other sister died shortly after.

I did not know anything about the adult Keiji, nor did I think about the fact that the author of the comic book was not, himself, a child. It did not occur to me that a child, experiencing the atomic bomb and its aftermath, could advance beyond what he had seen. Adulthood seemed like a betrayal of experience, letting childhood overgrow with—be swallowed by—the mirage-like ameliorations of time.

Sadako's story, meanwhile, could be seen as a coping mechanism contrived by adults. Her life and death were real—her belief and perseverance were real—but the inscribing of her story onto the frontispiece of history, especially in lieu of stories (testimonials, photographs) expressing, or attempting to express, the reality of a city being turned, in an instant, into a blazing, uninhabitable graveyard, felt—continues to feel—like a rush to closure, in the likeness of hope.

Keiji and Sadako served their purpose, in storytelling, as perspectives through which children were set against evil and made, against those odds, to bear the responsibility of how the atomic bombings would enter, and continuously reenter, history. It was as if the adults had abandoned the children, leaving them to not only process the horror, but to command its representation. Terror, privation, suffering, translated not through those closest to death—people with the least amount of time left to remember—but through those who would be traumatized longest.

The first site people visit when they visit the Peace Park is the Genbaku Dome, or the ruins of what was once the Hiroshima Prefectural Industrial Promotion Hall, on the east bank of the Motoyasu. The Motoyasu is one of seven tributaries of the Ota, up and down which tides carry the Inland Sea into and out of Hiroshima. The Genbaku Dome is more than its dome, but it is the dome—a skull, brain wholly evaporated—that everyone seeks out and remembers. It is surrounded, at all hours, in all seasons, by people from all over the world, all of whom, in proximity to the dome, slow down, as if caught in its gravity. The Genbaku Dome has become the most iconic bearer of the memory of August 6, 1945. Except it is neither a person nor people. It is, instead, the organization of people, therefore of memory. As the people who come from all over the world imagine the people inside the building, their imagination creates a form of theater in which not the dead but simulations of the living act out ritualized behaviors.

Very few visible ruins of the atomic bomb remain. People are not often characterized as ruins, even as their disintegration and enshrinement—as victims and more enduringly as survivors—unfolds coincident to them. The theater unfolds, more accurately, in the somnolent, ghostlike—even deer-like—behaviors of the people in the park, who surround the Genbaku Dome to try to make sense not only of what the ruin is articulating—now, in the present—but what they are, by being there.

I watched a pink boat, circular, like a small cake, motor up the Motoyasu. It was a tour boat with only two passengers: the tour guide and the tourist, both middle-aged Japanese women. They sat on opposite sides of the cake, facing each other. The tour guide was holding a microphone. They passed the Genbaku Dome, which became, in the gaze of the pink cake, an attraction in an amusement park. The tour guide's voice rose up the banks. Her voice, echoing, transformed the Genbaku Dome and its skeletal frame further, from an amusement park attraction into an abandoned sanitarium, engulfed by a city, a civilization that had little use for it, except as some kind of threatening reminder.

The Peace Park is a garden. There is the feeling that what is growing, what the garden is producing—every year, more elements are added to the solemn spectacle of grieving and remembrance—is yet to be determined.

A lawn mower could be heard through the trees. A man wearing a light blue jump suit and a white helmet over a backwards baseball cap, was mowing Domanju with a weed trimmer. A man in a motorized wheelchair, parked between two stone lanterns, revved his motor, then raced up to Domanju. He moved the stick shift of his wheelchair like he was writing. The motor whirred. A group of young women in white baseball caps stood at the base of Domanju, staring, with heads tilted, as if at a painting.

Domanju is a mound between the Honkawa and Motoyasu tributaries. The remains—the ashes, the relics—of 70,000 people killed by the atomic bomb are buried, safeguarded, in Domanju. It is a perfect circle around and rises out of the ground like an overgrown eye. An eye that can no longer see but is breathing, just beneath the first layer of earth. A breast, the crown of a bubble, the sun on the horizon, an atomic bomb's fireball at sixty milliseconds.

Mounds mark a fall. They are the graves of those who fell, were felled, as well as those who survived to deposit the remains and reseal the earth. The aspect of sleeping puts the dream first, which makes sleep the consequence of dreams, not vice versa.

A small stone sculpture, resembling the finial at the top of a pagoda, sits on top of Domanju. It emanates a radius of protection. The bomb (Little Boy) that was dropped on Hiroshima, the plane (Enola Gay) that conveyed it, the crew of the plane (including the son of the plane's namesake), the scientists and army officers and politicians who made and ordered and deployed it, the multifarious forms of what is known as *the enemy* on all sides of every ocean, homegrown, collective, hysteric, and/or bred in isolation, in every conceivable language, exist, in abstraction and in reality, in the sky. The sky, as I learned from *I Saw It*, harbors gods and demons at once and is the site, therefore, of a primary gamble in faith. That is, expectation.

I have visited Domanju three times: in 1988 (when I was ten); 2011 (on the 66th anniversary of the bombing, and my 33rd birthday); and 2016. It was not until 2016 that I noticed a door. On the north-facing side of Domanju, cut into the side of the mound, is a short staircase leading down to a metal door. The

door startled me. It bestowed an aspect of fantasy. It suggested a clandestine, unending world. An underground network, a labyrinth. Shadow Hiroshima. That behind the door stood either a single, self-contained object, like an inexplicable idol or letter, or a replication of the universe. These suggestions were ways for my mind to wander away from the fact of lives, entire families, being reduced, in one second, to ash, mounds of ash, over which the world continued to tread. Even though I thought I understood that the remains were material, and not merely a premise, for which Domanju was the figuration, I had not imagined that the mound could be entered. Because I had not imagined that a grave could be entered.

Who opened the door? Who entered the mound? In facing the door, I was facing the fact that I had taken Domanju to be a ritual, therefore symbolic, grave. And that because I had been introduced to the atrocity of the atomic bombings as a child, by children, I had taken everything to be symbolic. Everything had become a paper crane.

What is not the mound? What is not on the dark side of the door? A mound, surrounded by land, dreams of becoming an island, surrounded by water. Planted, at its summit, with a small shrine, reached by a staircase of stones, the first stone laid at the precise limit of the tide. As the moon continues to age, the limit rises, until only the roof of the small shrine remains.

Approximately 815 of the 70,000 people have been named. The remains of the other (approximately) 69,185 people—if it was or is possible to accurately enumerate lives from their ashes—include the namelessness that was one of the effects of the bomb: the extermination of life, the extermination of both the corpse and the name of that life.

What are the nameless people's names? If we knew their names, what would we do with them? We could begin to imagine the sound of their names being spoken by people who loved them.

## MIYAJIMA

We crossed two streams on our way up Mount Misen. Yasu said the sound of a mountain stream is seseragi. The man selling soda and ice cream at the top of the mountain was asleep. A small deer was resting near a large rock between a cypress and a cedar. To the north, Hiroshima Bay and the city of Hiroshima. To the east, islands forming shadows on the sea to the horizon. Somewhere in the sea was Kurahashi, the island where my grandfather and great-grandmother were born. I felt overly self-conscious, as if the island could see me. I turned several circles, to see if one island stood out. They all did. There were so many islands, so many shadows, I was sure I was looking not at my ancestral island but through it. My eyes were not ready. It had taken decades to visualize Hiroshima as a living, transcendent city curved along a bay, not an abstract shape attached to the weighted pronunciation of a name. It had taken decades to learn the seven rivers formed one, rising and falling with one tide. Hiroshima was a small light in an enormous cloud, the cloud periodically burning away to reveal the light even smaller and clouded from within, like a color that cannot be seen if stared at directly, only while looking away.

We descended the mountain. Crossed a bridge—painted vermilion to ward off evil—and returned to Itsukushima. It was early evening. The sun was going down across the Ondo Strait. We walked into the tide toward the torii gate. Seaweed was bright green on the sand. When the tide is high, the gate floats above water. The tide was low, going out.

We asked everyone we met in Hiroshima: *Are you going to the memorial?*

And everyone we met answered: *No.*

## SHIRAKAMI

Shirakami Shrine is on the northwest corner of Peace Boulevard and Rijo-dori. Shira is white, kami are divine spirits. In the age when Hiroshima cut a quicker descent to the sea, the northwest corner of Peace and Rijo-dori was a reef projecting into the bay. White paper was mounted on the reef to warn incoming ships.

A young woman was walking down Peace Boulevard. Her face was white. A waxy oil, then a white powder mixed with water into a paste, painted just short of her hairline. Her eyes were focused on the small mountain at the end of the boulevard. At the top of the mountain, in the trees, was a museum, which was showing (not that she could see it) Yoko Ono's *The Road of Hope*. A young man, standing on the sidewalk outside Shirakami Shrine, was staring into the viewfinder of a black camera. The young woman entered his view. He looked up, and stepped forward into the young woman's focus. He asked if he could take her picture. She hesitated. A moment of genial unease passed between them.

The camera opened a cave. The young woman approached. The mouth evoked the precise, watchful appetites of all life forms in the dark. The woman did not alter her expression but receded further into the whiteness of her face. The man took several photographs, rapidly, bowed, then the young woman passed on.

No record remains of shipwrecks on the reef. The shrine maintains the image of white paper spelling out a sequence not entirely dissimilar to surrender, by which incoming ships once gathered their strength, and floated, eyes closed, into Hiroshima.

## AUGUST 6, 2011

Every story, every testimonial, begins with it having been a day like any other. Blue sky, clear. But it was also a day like any other because it was a day in an endless series of days in which the sun rose, and the people with it, to war. Blue sky, clear, not because these are details of a day like any other, but because they were the final details.

At 8:15 and 15 seconds on the morning of August 6, 1945, a United States B-29 Superfortress dropped a uranium bomb on the city of Hiroshima on the island of Honshu. Little Boy exploded 1,903 feet above Shima Hospital, on the east bank of the Motoyasu River, incinerating, in less than a second, 80,000 people.

At 8:15 on the morning of August 6, 2011, a bell was struck in the Peace Park. The bell's reverberations were heavy and thick. 60,000 people in the park were spellbound, could not move. At 8:20, the mayor recited testimony from a woman who was sixteen at the time of the bombing:

*In that soundless world, I thought I was the only one left . . .*
*Suddenly, I heard lots of voices crying and screaming . . .*
*I did manage to move enough to save one young child . . .*

Then Masahiro Fukuhara and Nanoka Fujita mounted the stage. They were sixth graders—Masahiro at Misasa Elementary,

Nanoka at Koi Elementary—and had been chosen to be the children's representatives of the memorial ceremony. Their task was to deliver the Commitment to Peace. They stood side-by-side and fixed their eyes on the sky beyond the museum:

> *On March 11, countless lives were lost in the Tōhoku earthquake and tsunami. Even now, many people are still missing.*

Their voices were plangent, definitive. They sounded like they were delivering soliloquies at the edge of a cliff. I thought of the young boy standing up to the spirits of the peach orchard in Kurosawa's dream (*I can buy peaches at the store! But where can you buy a whole orchard in bloom?*) Masahiro and Nanoka's message was of sorrow and hope, but they were speaking to the ruins. Adults, what can adults provide? What can adults instill in the faithful and faithless alike that the thousands of disappeared and disappearing witnesses cannot? The morning was a ritual, but Masahiro and Nanoka, their voices pitched into the sky beyond the museum, reinforced the fact, by way of the sun and heat—eyes closed, sweating, clenching their fists—that we were gathered in a burial ground. It was as if they were saying: if *we* understand, if *we* are courageous enough to raise our voices above the bodies of the dead . . .

The basement auditorium of the Memorial Museum was full, but during the intermission between Japanese and English, it emptied, and only a small number of people remained. Ten westerners, Americans mostly, moved to the front to listen to five hibakusha—two women, three men—share their stories. I opened my notebook and wrote down as much as I could, because I knew I wanted—that I would continue to want—to return, every year, to their stories, to what they had come such an extraordinary distance to share.

Keiko was eight at the time of the bomb. She spoke the longest. Her story began with a refusal. People were dying all around her—burning, thirsty, in need of water. She gave them water from the family well. They drank the water, vomited, died. She knew she did not kill them but felt, *it was me!* It was easier for Keiko to take responsibility for their deaths than to try to explain what she could not. Her story began when she decided she was never going to tell anyone. She called it her *invisible scar*.

Isao was thirteen at the time of the bomb. Shoso and Keijiro were sixteen. Sumiko was seventeen. Shoso said he hated America. He took our hands in his and thanked us for being there. I felt in his hands the burden of his hatred yet saw on his face the complexity of his hatred being unresolved, solicitous, open.

Shoso Hirai (16)
*My father and younger brother were killed instantly . . . My older brothers were in China as soldiers . . . But the air raid alarm was soon cancelled . . . As soon as I touched the door, I was hit by a strong blast . . . It became dark all around me . . . Every path that led to my house was engulfed in flames . . . I thought, There must have been a big disaster in Hiroshima . . . We spent the night at the farmer's house . . . It seemed as if we had just walked through the Gate of Hell . . . We carried my father's bones back home.*

Sumiko Hirosawa (17)
*But at this moment, everybody is happy now . . . But, everything had to go away anyway . . . But, what did you want to know? . . . But, everything is okay now . . . It was a long time, but it was okay . . . It took a long time to make the rice and the vegetables, and they came to pick them up . . . It was the farmers that took care of everybody . . . We had to help ourselves, but it was okay, we had the farmers.*

Keijiro Matsushima (16)

*That springtime, my father died . . . Beautiful, shining in the morning sun, white-silver planes . . . The whole world turned to something like an orange world, a sunset world . . . I felt like I had just been thrown into an oven . . . Hundreds, hundreds of thunders at the same moment . . . No one screamed, no voice, no sound . . . I was just crawling around on the floor . . . Everyone felt one bomb was dropped here beside me . . . Their hair had stood up straight, charcoal-gray skin, and their clothes were torn and singey . . . I could see red muscles under the peeled skin . . . Their faces were like baked pumpkins . . . Exactly a procession of ghosts . . . They were still able to walk, that's good . . . For many days these bodies were floating in the river, up and down, with the movement of the tides . . . Real hell . . . Real hell . . . I decided to leave Hiroshima, and I wanted to go to my mommy's home . . . My whole city of Hiroshima is dying, maybe I was a little sentimental at the moment . . . I began walking to my mommy's home in the farm country . . . So, you can tell a man's fate . . . And even today, there are many old women who couldn't get married, they are living very lonely lives . . . Well, that's almost all I experienced, so I say that's all . . . I had read an article in Boys Magazine about A-bomb, and as I was crossing the bridge, I thought about that article . . . I was a smart kid, but it didn't help . . . I will also have to disappear soon.*

Isao Aratani (13)

*Sweet potatoes were planted there, and we went to pull weeds . . . We heard an unusually loud propeller sound . . . Two or three parachutes . . . Heard the sound of full-speed engine . . . At the same time we were blown off the ground . . . We didn't have any idea what had happened . . . Sky-scraping mushroom-shaped cloud . . . Walked like ghost . . . Skin had slipped . . . One of my classmates gave water to several victims, all of them died soon after saying Thank you . . . We tried to escape deadly exposure to the sunshine, which increased our pain . . . They tried to cool themselves by the rain, they drank the rain . . .*

Immediately after the bombing, 8:15 a.m., it was high tide, and the water was deep . . . They supplied food such as crackers and rice balls . . . The city was burned and reduced to ash in one night . . . And couldn't even tell if the bodies belonged to man or woman . . . They died while standing . . . I remember the smell of cremation . . . We had a complicated feeling about the defeat, and also relief . . . We didn't want to talk about our memories for many years . . . The Poplar Tree Will Transfer the Story from Generation to Generation.

Keiko Ogura (8)

I am the youngest who still remembers that day . . . Every year I stand on the riverbank . . . There were a bunch of bananas and oranges . . . My mother sold her wedding ring to the army . . . Americans had a tall nose . . . Shiny . . . Children had to bite [edible grasses] 100 times . . . They heard a kind of rumor that near Hiroshima City there had been a big fire . . . At midnight they tried to escape from the temple . . . That was the time the teacher decided to tell the children about the atomic bomb . . . Look at the Buddha—can you see all the faces behind the Buddha? Your parents are already in heaven . . . Only this year did I ask my brother how he spent his days in the temple . . . I want you to understand the invisible scars of the survivors, the invisible sorrows . . . I would like to tell my invisible scars from now on . . . On August the 7th I climbed up the hill near my house and saw the city . . . Behind the city I saw Ujina Port and the Seto Inland Sea . . . Everybody will be the victim soon . . . I want to say, I am sorry, we have the same destiny . . . I feel we are all connected by the sea . . . We couldn't have time to sleep . . . We stayed up all night . . . All Hiroshima people were so sleepy that morning . . . Finally, my mother said, I want to die at home, not in a shelter . . . Father had lucky inspiration . . . I was hit on the road . . . I woke up in darkness, pitch darkness . . . So quiet . . . The thatched farmer's house started to burn . . . Oily, gray, charcoal-colored rain . . . It was so sticky . . . There were so many traces of black rain everywhere in my house . . . It goes together for awhile, and then there *was a curve . . . He wanted to follow the plane . . . He could see from the top of the hill, the top of the cloud, and its color was pink . . . It aches a lot to touch your body, so not to touch your body . . . I could smell the smell of burnt hair . . . The other side the victims there could barely move, they were moving so slowly . . . They died, squatting in a line on the road, on the stone steps . . . That was the beginning of my invisible scars . . . And that moment I decided not to tell my story to anyone . . . Everywhere there were hundreds of big flies . . . In the afternoon, they stopped moving their hands, and they were covered in black flies . . . And then I could see the Inland Sea, and it seemed so near, because there was nothing . . . We have a strong fear about our genetic problems . . . As soon as I saw the shiny wings of the Enola Gay, I was frozen, I started to cry . . .*

We sat on the stone embankment above the Motoyasu, our legs hanging over the water, the Genbaku Dome behind us. Thousands of people sat along the embankment. The water was dark, except for where it was illuminated by paper lanterns. There were thousands of lanterns. The volume of love was concentrated in their colors. Prayers were written on each lantern: the names of loved ones, ancestors. Then the lanterns were sent into the river. Each held a small flame. The lanterns, in their slow, tentative movements, became a community. Pink, tangerine, lavender, light blue, watermelon. They gathered and slid against each other. The sea pulled.

Pumpkin-yellow lanterns floated beneath our feet. Silent, bound together with the countenance of a family making its evening rounds, each member decorated with hearts, red suns, birds, stripes of color. The family of lanterns, moving in one long streak, and gathering beneath the bridge, resembled a hive, each family member guttering out, until fully extinguished, the souls of the dead taking leave of their performance in the ceremony. Would the fires burn through the night?

## TOHOKU

An old woman planted spinach in the ruins of her house. Where her house once stood was now rubble and dirt: metal, wood, ceramic roof tiles, cloth, shredded rush. She made a clearing in the shape her house used to make. The woman's house was demolished by a tsunami that pushed through the coast, bringing everything between itself and the dry world along with it. The woman was planting spinach in the shape of her house, though her house was demolished and spread beyond where it had stood. The spinach, the shape, was where the woman could go to be with her house. Planting spinach in the grave of a house seemed a gesture. Who would eat the spinach? Would the old woman eat it? Would there be enough for her to eat? Would she share it with her neighbors?

Her neighbors were gone. Their houses were also demolished and spread. Some of her neighbors were dead.

The woman was wearing light-colored jeans, wide in the leg, a windbreaker, white with pink cuffs, and an enormous white hat that curled around her head like the cap of a mushroom. The tsunami reached heights over 130 feet and pushed through the coast six miles inland.

A mushroom expanded on a tree. Small fish leaped over larger fish. Small crabs came out of holes. The holes closed, the ground pulled from below by an invisible tide. The woman buried each spinach plant above its first leaves. She was replanting her house. The spinach shall be the foundation. When it grows, I shall return. I will again have a place to live.

One of the woman's neighbors, a man, was among the dead. He had asked her to accompany him for tea. She had said no. She had some idea of heaven that precluded losing one's focus in life.

There was no focus. Life was full of disregard.

The man returned to the woman in a dream. She was squatting in a field, pulling plants out of the ground. No end of plants. She never moved, but they kept coming to her hand. Suddenly she could feel, over her right shoulder, the presence of a man. His presence was that of a warm, wet animal. She wanted to look but could not. The presence of the man became breath. Burning hair and salt and something like spiced gourd. She relaxed. The breath had a voice, and the voice said, *You will put everything back. Only then will you be able to leave.* There was no longer any man, but the voice was unquestionably the voice of a man. By then her neighbor, the man, had already died. Some part of their houses, demolished and spread, had commingled a mile away from where they had lived.

The sky was blowing, beating light through shoals of smoke and fog. The landscape was a wasteland, resembling a landfill, a war-ravaged city, a militarized zone, a clear-cut, a desert. Piles of brush, gutted buildings, crushed cars, boats on rooftops, imprints of houses, massive entanglements of wire and wood, rotten and undifferentiated.

Are ghosts anomalous to the rule of life? They remind us that life is a compositional process, with seams and fissures between moments. The seams and fissures allow for ghosts to emerge—through the rage, regret, foreclosure, the infinite spoils of the soul of the living. If death is the rule, ghosts become the living. Do the living then become the anomaly?

The old woman lived alone. The house had been lively, there were more people, a family, but the shadows grew longer, darker, each threshold worn smooth. Liveliness caught on the webs, let out the windows. The man, who once walked the street on which both of their houses sat, wearing a blue shirt and looking, to her, like a man who had something on his mind, but hiding it, hiding it inside the look of a man with nothing at all on his mind, a spore on the wind, aloof to the earth, a room without walls, the wind sowing emptiness before it.

## MARGARET ICHINO

Dear Margaret Stanicci,

My name is Brandon Shimoda. I am trying to find a woman with the maiden name of Margaret Ichino. She was married to my grandfather, Midori Shimoda, in 1941. I am wondering if you might be her. I am gathering information about my grandfather's life leading up to the war. I know of Margaret through his FBI file, which cites the dates of their marriage. I am hoping to connect with her, as she is the only living person who might have some memory of this time in my grandfather's life.

I am also interested to learn more about Margaret. I recently watched a video interview with her conducted at Manzanar. I was surprised at the possibility that this might be the same Margaret. I attempted to contact Margaret through her niece. She was able to pass along my appeal, but the communication ended there. My grandfather passed away in 1996.

If you are the Margaret Ichino/Stanicci I am referring to, I would be deeply grateful to hear from you. If not, my sincere apologies. I am living in Tucson, Arizona. My phone number is 406-241-1980 and my email address is brandonshimoda@gmail.com. I have included a picture of myself, so that you know I am an actual person; the photo was taken this summer in Kumamoto, Japan.

A phone rang on a cul-de-sac. I was pacing the train tracks near downtown Santa Fe. I had called several numbers corresponding to the two addresses where I mailed the above letter a year before. One of the letters came back. The other did not. I reached busy signals, dial tones. The addresses I had for Margaret were in Santa Fe. The fifth call connected. I prepared myself. I had watched a three-hour video interview with Margaret, given to me by the historian at Manzanar, in which she talked at length about her life before and after the war, and I had memorized her response to the question, *Where were you on December 7, 1941?*

*Yes, that was interesting . . . Because I remember things that happened*, she began. Margaret and Midori married March 26, 1941, Midori's birthday. According to Midori's FBI file, they separated December 1941. No reason is given, though the file adds, *No children were forthcoming from this union.* Margaret, in her long, halting response to where she was on December 7, 1941, does not mention having been married.

A woman answered. It was the voice of the woman from the interview.

*Hello, is this Margaret Stanicci?*

*No*, the woman answered, *you have the wrong number.*

When I explained who I was and how I found the number, she hesitated, then said: *Oh yes, I've heard about you.*

Then she said: *This is Margaret's friend. I thought you might be calling . . .*

I reiterated what I wrote a year earlier, but instead of naming Margaret as Midori's first wife, I said they had been friends, and that because Margaret was the only living person that knew Midori in the years before the war, it was important I talk with her, could she put me in touch?

*It was so long ago*, she said. *I doubt my friend Margaret would remember.*

I told her I was in Santa Fe and would be grateful for an opportunity to meet Margaret. She asked if I had visited the Palace of the Governors or the History Museum or if I knew about the camp (the Department of Justice prison) on the hill where 4,555 Japanese men had been imprisoned (March 1942–April 1946), or if I had visited Rosario Cemetery, where two of the prisoners were buried. M. Sudo (d. January 3, 1945) and D. Yoshikawa (d. June 6, 1945), both buried in the rose garden. I said I had visited the ruins of the prison, that I would go to the cemetery, and that I had watched a three-hour interview with Margaret and was fascinated by her life and especially how, after incarceration, she devoted herself to the study of Japanese culture. She became silent, then said: *It was a difficult time in her life . . . She doesn't want to talk about it.*

I knew she was Margaret but did not let on, thinking she might slip, reveal something. She knew enough about how

Margaret felt to reveal the pain of remembering. If she was going to continue to play Margaret's friend, I was going to continue pretending I did not know that she was Margaret. It was easier for her to deflect by being someone else, but not so easy to simply hang up. When I told her that I had visited Manzanar and found the spot where Margaret's barracks had been—

```
No. 1,900 ICHINO, Margaret Taki
Family No. 21061
D.O.B. 12/28/18
Marital Status: D
Date of Original Entry: 6/1/42
Date of Final Departure: 5/10/45
Destination of Final Departure: Chicago, IL
Type of Original Entry: MnAC
Type of Final Departure: Ind-Invit
Pre-Evacuation Address: LA, CA
Block/Building No. 32-3-3
```

—she became silent again, maybe a little afraid. What kind of ghost was I? It was not that Margaret Ichino was married to Midori for a few irrecoverable months seventy years earlier, but that she existed in a parallel life entirely, a life in which I was never born.

I wanted Margaret's friend to tell Margaret I called. It would have upheld the illusion of her game and confirmed that, yes, you found me. But instead she kept slipping into her friend's rueful voice. I wondered if she and Midori talked again—after their separation, the war, after each had remarried. They both moved to New York City. Margaret married a man named George, whom she mentioned, in the interview, having dated before December 1941. I had been told that Midori had been married before and that he walked in on his first wife with another man. Was George the man he walked in on? That was the story, anyway, which seemed to me an expeditious way of dispensing with a more complicated history, while casting an unnamed woman as the villain.

I kept thanking her for being so open in talking with a stranger, especially on behalf of Margaret. When I said, *You haven't told me your name*, she said, *There's someone at the door . . . I have to go*, and she hung up.

**Margaret (Ichino) Stanicci:** A lot of individuals did have unresolved feelings of resentment or bitterness or anger. You had to work it through. And I worked it through conscientiously. It took two years. Two years was the breaking of . . . I had to work through a lot. And I realized a lot of people had not. That some of them, in their later lives . . . something did trigger it, and they had to do something with it. Some went into a new form of activism or resolved it in other ways. If you, didn't, it just stayed inside you as a negative binding force.

**Richard Potashin (Manzanar):** *How did you work it, though?*

When I got out and thought about it, I said, I was put into a camp as an American citizen, which is against the Constitution. It was because of my ancestry, and I know absolutely nothing about my ancestry, very little about the family, nothing about the culture, nothing except what you gather through reading, just generally, or in school. So I thought to go back to college and focus on Japan. I was drawn to the New School. They were particularly concerned with the German situation. They tried to pull out as many German Jews as they could. Many of their professors were German and some of their students too. They were good students more serious than in Los Angeles. They came from Europe, so they had a different tradition.

So I wrote and mentioned that I had just come out of the camps. They were very sympathetic and gave me a full scholarship [laughs]. For every class I wrote a paper on Japan. In sociology, I wrote a paper on the camps and a lady who had been in one of the German camps and had gotten out . . . I don't know how they got out . . . I mentioned that one of the psychological effects I recognized in camp was this, what shall I . . . the collapsing of your universe. So the things you were interested in, the things you were involved in and aware of, things that you were doing, had been eliminated and condensed. And the conversation from the beginning became more constricted, and eventually it was like: what is the best mess hall to go to today? It was discussion on that level which shocked me because they were persons of education. There was this tremendous constriction, and it was only when you were able to get . . . I don't know, if something started you on something and if there was a little group that could focus on something, you had a discussion. But the whole atmosphere was really a lessening of a human being.

Anyway, I wrote as many papers as I could, looking at Japan. I was learning. Then it was time to write a thesis, and the only thing I haven't looked at is religion. So I thought, I'll explore religion. What was the source of my mother's inner strength? In psychology we studied the theory of frustration breeds aggression, and I said, that's true of most people, but it wasn't with my mother. She had nothing but frustration in her life, a tremendous amount, yet there was no aggression. A young child can always feel a shift in the parents' emotional energies. If there had been any aggression I would have felt it.

I did a year of reading Confucianism, Shinto, Buddhism, and decided to focus on Zen because they had so much influence in Japanese culture. I started to read, and I couldn't understand a thing. Which was very interesting because how is it that I can know what every word means, I read the whole sentence, I know they're pointing to something, they're trying to say something, but I don't know what they're talking about? [Laughs] So I went to the New York Public Library every day and wrote notes. I don't know how many pages of notes. Suzuki was teaching at Columbia, probably the first teacher of Zen at that time. Very few books had been translated. I had a difficult time.

Then, one day, I had an experience in which I think I could understand what they were talking about. If that was so, then it was an experience, you see, of energy. It was like, I think the universe is really . . . there was a love pervading; it was an energy universe.

*Where were you on December 7, 1941?*

Yes, that was interesting . . . Because I remember things that happened. But I was not in touch with the Japanese community and . . . but I had dated. I was trying to think of when did I date. I had dated George Stanicci once before and I also, and I had dated some others too. But I had lost track of everybody. And, and then when I heard about what happened, it, it just gave me such a shock. And I had done some, done some artwork on my own and there was, let me see, what was it? A poem . . . it's, it's something like "When winter comes, can spring be far behind?" Do you remember that poem? If I remember that part that had that . . . so I went up on Hollywood Boulevard and decided to make a card. And, and I sketched, well, I bought a piece of acetate and sketched and, you know, engraved a little card. And it had a barren tree, it was this tree, and some, some crosses, and, but, and that, that was it. You see, this was going to be winter, but there would be spring. And I remember that was the card that I sent out to friends. And then I didn't want to be left alone because I was, my family had gone since they had already been evacuated in their section of the city. So I asked my friend, one of my friends that was in the girls club with me when I was younger, and, and we still kept in touch. It was, as a matter of fact, we were active. And it was called, the girls club was actually called Rho Sigma Rho. But, so that's, so I asked to stay with her, and she lived right next to George Stanicci that I had dated before, once anyway, and I thought that would be nice because at least I would know one person and, you know, and her family. So I stayed with her, but then her parents, I guess were . . . friends of their parents wanted them to move to another place in order to go to a different, I don't know, place. So, so she and her family moved out, and I was living in her house alone.

*You mentioned your family had been evacuated. Where did they go?*

They went to Manzanar.

*How did you feel?*

When our time came, we were evacuated, so I knew that whole section of town was going. I found out the next morning when I got up and got ready to go that my neighbor's mother had stayed up to scrub the kitchen floor of the house they were renting and . . . How could you spend your time scrubbing a kitchen floor before you were getting ready to leave? As nisei, I don't think we would have had that inclination.

Last night I was in one of the discussion groups. There was a lady whose ancestors came from Finland. I mentioned the incident about my neighbor scrubbing the kitchen floor. She said she was so delighted because her great-grandmother did exactly the same thing in Finland when the Russians were coming. They knew the Russians were coming and had been burning all the houses. And she heard that her great-grandmother scrubbed the floors and put out flowers.

We went on the old dusty train. They pulled them out of

storage because all the other trains were being used to move the troops. There were old gaslight fixtures. The seats were very dusty. They did give us a little lunch box; mine had a sandwich and an apple. We got off this train eventually in Lone Pine, then were transferred to a bus. We sat near the back. When we were coming close to Manzanar, the bus driver said, *You should be with your family and friends.* As you come off there's little groupings of probably eight or so that go into one room. Here I was alone, and my friend George and his mother would be two more. That's three, because we would be together, and I didn't know anyone. So he looked around the bus and saw two friends of his and ran up to them and said, *Would you like to join our group,* and they said, *Yes,* because they were alone. So they joined our group, and we were very small group of one, two, three, four, five. We were concerned whether we would have to have another family, but they decided we could be in one room. George and Grace Sasaki had just gotten married not long before, and that was a shame to spend their first year in Manzanar with two other families. We hung blankets, but that was not very sufficient.

*Do you remember your state of mind when you heard about the evacuation?*

I said, there's a possibility our parents would be put into a camp or taken because they're issei and they are aliens because they could never apply for citizenship. Since they were denied citizenship, they're obviously aliens and now they would be considered enemy aliens.

*First Japan attacks your country. You're an American. Then your country decides you're the enemy, 'cause you're Japanese. Now it sounds like you're trying to figure out how that comes together. How did you relate Zen with the war atrocities? How were you able to put any of this together?*

Only in the larger context. Not in terms of specifics. The deep part of Zen is you go into what they call the silence or the void. It's been translated *nothingness*. But it isn't nothingness. It's no-thing-ness. It's no-thing. What it is, is energy. Pure energy. And it's energy of different qualities. It's almost like you have spectrum after spectrum of energy. And each has qualities. That's where the universality of religions comes, which is something I'm pursuing now. But in terms of . . . There didn't . . . I don't think there had to be any . . . See, you don't have to analytically or rationally . . . Some things you cannot understand. As a matter of fact, quantum comes much closer. That was the first thing I realized in terms of quantum, which I had to work on because it's like, okay they had that either/or bit. We had been taught right along Aristotelian either/or. Yet now we were asked to say, it's both/and. How are you going do that? And I said, Okay, let's see how we can do it without the either/or, if they're both/and. And you have to work a different way.

*And that helped you understand how Japan and America came at odds and how you came in the middle of that?*

No, you don't have to anymore. [Laughs] You don't have to anymore.

It just happened.

It's like in the evolution of an individual, of a nation, of a larger grouping, eventually the evolution of a total world, you say. And you go through your growing stages. Every one has to go through the growing stages. And we have not arrived there yet.

## MONUMENT VALLEY

So I guess just start with . . .

*Evacuation?*

Right, when the Japanese were informed . . .

*The time they had to get out of California by . . . it was the beginning of March 1942. Midori left his studio in Pasadena to his assistant, a man named Jenkins, because he didn't have any money. A few years later, we heard he had killed his wife's lover and then himself.*

What about his wife?

*I think she's still alive . . .*

*Anyway, he left Pasadena in a burgundy coupe. He took Setsuko and his niece May, and they drove during the night, and during the day they just . . . laid low. I don't know where they hid the car . . . off road, I guess. It was wartime, and you didn't know what people would do.*

Midori had opened a small photography studio in Pasadena and was making money by taking pictures for department store catalogs and college yearbooks. He became friends with the yearbook editor at Pomona College, a boy named Jones. Jones's family had a turkey farm in Monticello, Utah. *You'll be safe*, he insisted. They packed clothes, toiletries, and a chest in which they carried their mother's silverware. Everything else was sold or turned over to friends or neighbors.

Monticello was settled in the 1880s by Mormons, on

occupied Navajo land. It was named after Thomas Jefferson's plantation in Virginia. There was a post office, gas station, courthouse, and a uranium mill. It was originally a vanadium mill but began to produce, during the war, a vanadium–uranium mix that was sent to Los Alamos, New Mexico. The mill and surrounding land were designated a National Defense Area. Locals described yellow dust on the grass, laundry stiffening and cracking, disintegrating off the line. Children went swimming in the pond downstream from the mill and rode horses and took naps in the tailings. No one knew what the yellow dust was. No one thought to connect it to the mill.

According to the Environmental Protection Agency's Superfund Program, 424 properties in Monticello were contaminated with radioactive tailings. According to an assessment made in 1986 by the EPA, the Department of Energy and the Utah Department of Environmental Quality, the contaminated properties were all near the uranium mill. The site was added to the National Priorities List on June 10, 1986. Cleanup began October 15, 1989 and was completed September 2, 1999. A total of 152,000 cubic yards of material was removed and relocated to a repository a mile down the road. The EPA deleted the site from the National Priorities List on February 28, 2000.

*Everyone in this town dies of cancer*, the owner of the pizzeria said. We were standing on the sidewalk. There was one traffic light and a girl holding a dog. *We had to shut the pizzeria down for a year because the septic tank was backed up with radioactive waste*, she said. *See those kids riding their bikes up the street from the Department of Public Safety? That's where the mill is*. It is a park now, with one long, loping path encircling a dry pond overgrown with tall cattails and reeds.

From a letter dated September 1, 1943, written by Dan B. Shields, district attorney for the State of Utah, to Edward J.

Ennis, director of the Alien Enemy Control Unit of the Department of Justice in Washington D.C., addressing the activities of Midori Arthur Shimoda, Department of Justice File #146-13-2-77-245:

This young man came to Utah at the time of the evacuation from California. He is a photographer by trade and an alien by birth. When he came to Utah he did a peculiar thing. He left the rather populous portions of the state and went down into the southeast corner to the town of Monticello, where he was the only Japanese, and there engaged in his photographic operations. He had been there but a short time when he succeeded in making trouble for himself.

DEVAUGHN JONES informed reporting Agent on July 28, 1942 that he had brought Subject to Monticello, Utah to assist his son in running a turkey farm. The townspeople inflamed by hate of the Japanese race in general threatened to lynch the Subject. No personal animosity brought this state of affairs.

To protect his sister who was with him at the time, Subject under persuasion from Mr. JONES agreed to leave Monticello, and go to Blanding, Utah where he obtained board and lodging at the residence of O.P. HURST which he paid for by working on the HURST farm. JONES advised that he was favorably impressed by Subject and was sorry that he had to "let him go." When Mr. JONES was advised that SHIMODA had "made quite a hit" with the people of Blanding, he inferred that the people of Blanding were of an essentially trusting nature, and that inasmuch as they had rarely seen a "city slicker" before they could be fooled quite easily. He

continued that while he had nothing of a de-
rogatory nature to say about SHIMODA and would
like to have kept him as his son's helper, he
nevertheless felt that being a Japanese, he
could bear watching.

According to the second volume of *Blanding City Centennial's Family Histories, 1905–2005*, Oscar Hurst *became aware of three Japanese children who needed a place to stay, a boy 18, his sister about 12 and a niece about 8. He brought them home and gave them shelter for a few months. Retta and Oscar were just about run out of the county for this act of kindness.* The three Japanese children were Midori, Setsuko, and May, the daughter of their oldest brother Setsuo. Midori was in his early thirties, Setsuko in her early twenties, and May in her late-teens, but the Mormons were able to convince themselves of the innocence of the Japanese by appraising them as children.

Oscar had nine children. He was the grandson of a polygamist exile. His grandfather fled with his three wives their imagined State of Deseret for Mexico, where he opened a sawmill. One day, a log came flying off the chute and crushed his skull. *There he was in his unmarked grave, and I felt quite guilty about it*, Oscar said. The wandering, immaculate guilt of a grandson. Oscar sought a correlation between his family's exile and the flight of the Japanese children. He found it in the government's persecution of people bound by religious conviction. To his mind, being Japanese was the equivalent of being from an outcast religion.

Blanding had once been called Grayson, after Joseph A. Lyman's wife Nellie, whose middle name was Grayson. It was the most populous town in San Juan County. The Navajo made up more than half of the county population. Before and during the war, the Bureau of Indian Affairs killed off the Navajo's sheep, which had formed the basis of their economy. The government emptied Navajo land by forcing the Navajo off the reservation for work. The Mormons, with their vision of the tabernacle of their minds illuminating the desert, were the beneficiaries.

*They lived a very simple life,* June wrote, *bringing cows home from the pasture, gathering eggs, picking vegetables, cleaning out the barn and chicken coop. Midori learned to ride a horse, took a lot of rides into the desert. They always had homemade bread and butter, corn with sliced tomatoes, chicken, lots of venison.*

*As a Mormon Mr. Hurst was not supposed to smoke, drink. But one of the highlights of their day was to share cigarettes after dinner on the front porch, cleaning their guns.*

The Alien Enemies Act was one of four anti-immigrant bills signed into law in 1798. Three of the bills were eventually repealed. The Alien Enemies Act of July 6, 1798, authorizing the arrest, incarceration, and deportation, of enemy aliens in a time of war, still stands. On December 7, 1941, within minutes of the attack on Pearl Harbor, FDR resurrected the Alien Enemies Act through Proclamation 2525, which targeted *all natives, citizens, denizens or subjects of Empire of Japan being of the age of fourteen years and upwards who shall be within the United States or within any territories in any way subject to the jurisdiction of the United States and not actually naturalized, who for the purpose of this Proclamation and under such sections of the United States Code are termed alien enemies.* The Proclamation imposed strict regulations on their movement and on what the Japanese were allowed to possess (subject to seizure and forfeiture), including:

*j. Cameras.*

*k. Papers, documents or books in which there may be invisible writing.*

From a signed statement dated September 3, 1943:

I MIDORI SHIMODA voluntarily give the following signed statement to WALTER W. FOLEY, JR.
of my own free will without threat or promise
knowing that I do not have to.

During the latter part of May I took a trip
with LYNN LYMAN to Monument Valley a distance
of 50 or 75 miles without a travel permit. I
went to meet a friend of mine. While there I
took several pictures with a speed graphic.
Those pictures were of Indians.

I had a Streamline <u>Browning</u> Camera and another <u>Browning</u> camera in my room. I knew they
should not be in the room but DEVON HURST
brought them in so I just let them stay.

I have read the above statement and it is
true and correct and I expect to testify to
the same.

Concerning paragraph (4).

I had written specifically about the son of
Mr. HURST having his brownie camera in this
room—we occupy the same bed-room.

I have not notified the local board that I
am separated from my wife—at present I am in
class 3-A in the Army—I have been negligent by
not notifying the proper authority.

<u>from SUMMARY OF FACTS AND OPINIONS</u>
Subject's appearance before the Board is due
to his apparent possession of a camera. This
boy is physically frail, but of an artistic
and very sensitive nature. He is high strung.
He had difficulty in restraining tears. He
feels discouraged. He came to America when he
was nine years old. He states that it is difficult for him to look at himself as an alien.
He was educated in Pasadena. He completed

Junior College there. Took an art course while in school and became intensely interested in the chemistry of photography and pursued that activity in a technical and art school until he became very expert indeed. He evidently loves that work and can make a good living out of it.

It appears that the only camera he had in his possession which he owned was a 5x7 Curtis Color Camera, which the Pasadena police permitted him to retain. The other cameras he had to do with belonged to Mr. Biggs or Mr. Devon Hurst or to Mr. Evans. Certainly none of his conduct bears a remote relation to anything subversive. Blanding is far from the maddening crowd. It is a remote agricultural and cattle raising community far in the southeastern corner of the state; has few people—far from any railroad or any defense or war activities. It has no saloons, and not even beer is sold there. It is a country of magnificent distances. Subject said it seemed so rural and so peaceful and free that it was hard to remember that he was an alien.

Subject is married but separated. No children. He did not notify his draft board of his change of status. He seems sincere when he says he very willing to go into the Army and although he is not strong, having on two occasions nursed himself back to health of a protracted illness, thinks he could very useful to the Army in his own field. He represents one of the many individual tragedies of the war. We think he is not in the least dangerous.

We recommend that he be paroled under sponsorship as soon as possible so that his spirit may not be broken.

Late afternoon. Midori is standing on a hill in Monument Valley. He is facing north. In front of him is West Mitten Butte. Across the valley in the distance is the Bear and the Rabbit, Castle Butte, the King on His Throne, Big Indian, Brigham's Tomb, and Sentinel Mesa. Behind him is Mitchell Mesa, named after Ernest Mitchell, a prospector last seen entering a silver mine. Mitchell's body was later recovered at the base of the mesa, two vertical striations of bright light illuminating his face.

The genuine spectacle of the monuments begins in the evening, when shadows stretch across the valley. When the shadows touch, the valley is deprived of color, which feels truer to the disequilibrium and degradation of the land and its people. The monuments are liberated from the glare of the sun and the gaze of strangers. They remake themselves out of time.

The moon is bright. An emotional core is released in the colorlessness. Beauty is at its peak when no one is looking.

The monuments are isolated. Long, vertical discolorations evince successions of up-thrust, exposure. The King on His Throne is homely. Casts the people in the role of followers, whereas he is the one who knows nothing, who cannot fathom what he is facing. Standing at the bow of his ship, archipelagoes of land rising, the human face and body reverting to sandstone, from which to touch, to carve, a new face and body, wind in the twenty-first century.

The incarceration and complete obliteration of a soul. What name would you give to that spectacle?

It is not until I read, on a display in the small museum at the edge of the monuments, that *deities, animals, and the ancestors of today's humans emerged from below through a giant reed* that I appreciate the sadness of this landscape. Tsé Bii' Ndzisgaii: valley of the rocks.

One of Midori and Devon's favorite places was a swimming hole in Bluff, twenty-five miles down the road from Blanding. When I asked one of the locals where it was, she said, *kaput*, but I figured the hole itself had to still be there. It was tucked into a small, crescent-shaped canyon, thick with cattails and reeds. From out of their thickness, a fox appeared. It trotted onto the levee, then, seeing us, hastened toward the canyon wall. When it reached the wall, other foxes appeared, each fox on a different ledge. I thought of an advent calendar or the face of a clock, a door behind each hour opening. The foxes looked at us, then disappeared, one-by-one, into the wall. All but the first fox. It started climbing the wall, ran along a ledge, then leaped to another ledge, then another, higher and higher up the wall. It rose like smoke, until it was lost among the ledges.

Devon worked at the uranium mill in Monticello. One day, he borrowed Midori's car. Everyone in town knew the Japanese man's burgundy coupe. It was always parked on the corner of South 300 West and West 400 South. Then it was spotted at the mill and immediately reported to the authorities.

Three years later, Devon was in a spotter plane above Japan when the atomic bomb was dropped on Hiroshima. Did he think of Midori as he watched the mushroom cloud climbing out of the sun?

*My father has always felt responsible for your grandfather's arrest,* Nancy, Devon's daughter, said. We were standing in the small lobby of the motel she owned. The war was over by the time Nancy was born, but its interpretation, with which she was indoctrinated, was only beginning to unfold.

One of the first things she mentioned were the grapes on the arbor at her grandparents' house. *My grandmother's grape juice was delicious,* she said. I pictured grape vines spiraling like barbed wire around the corpses of two charitable Mormons. *Mormons are compassionate people,* Nancy said. *They love everyone.*

Then she said: *The Second Coming is soon. Three prophets will die on the streets of the Middle East and be resurrected on the spot. They're coming to kill us.* She was exuberant, talking fast. Who's coming to kill us? The three prophets? *Children from Mexico. They're gangs, you know. But we're not afraid. We have guns.* The tableau of Oscar cleaning his guns in front of the Japanese children rematerialized as a foreboding rehearsal of the hallucinatory horror of white power. *And when Jesus returns, there will be one thousand years of peace on earth. We'll be reunited with our ancestors.* But isn't it safe here? *Yes, very safe.* So then isn't it already peaceful? *Yes, but a massive earthquake is going to hit Salt Lake City and split the country in half: north and south.* The desire for catastrophe seemed desperate, religious—a religious desperation both a consequence and a betrayal of the surrounding emptiness, the complete insulation inside of which the people were living and rotting.

I thought of how compassion and goodwill are translated down generations. How good faith acts are converted into stories that are told to children and grandchildren as a way to dispossess the subjects of their agency, turn them into objects, keep them marginalized and at the whim and motive of power. Nancy asked if we wanted to spend the night at the motel, for free, and showed us a small room behind the lobby. An unmade cot was pushed up against a cream-colored cement brick wall. Was this a family tradition? I imagined what it would be like to spend a night on the cot. I imagined grape juice streaming down the wall, pooling in the sheets. I thought of how her xenophobia must have been informed, through some convoluted yet absolutely mandated translation, by the stories she heard about the three Japanese children her grandparents took in. I thought of the three Japanese children and the children crossing the border, and, five or six hundred miles from the border, Mormons, rabid, ravenous, armed.

*Mormons love everyone*, she said again. *We love everyone.* She did not seem sad or lost or like she was trying to convince herself that the compassion by which she claimed to have been birthed was real. It was, to her, demonstrably real. She was entirely in her element, of her element, informed by and happily in debt and deference to her element.

*I was two when my grandfather died*, Nancy said. He died in 1954. (Devon died, of silicosis, in 2012.) *I was the last person my grandfather saw. He called for me, and I climbed onto the bed. I'm excited to meet him*, she said. *I'm excited to meet my grandfather.*

It took me a moment to understand what she meant. I looked up at the sky. The dark cloud covering Monticello evoked the underside of a garden, its flowers and vegetables and fruits abundant and growing into the sky above the cloud, yet invisible to us in the motel parking lot.

As we were leaving, Nancy, smiling, became serious, looked directly at me, and said: *Aren't you excited to meet your grandfather?*

Department of Justice

UNITED STATES ATTORNEY
DISTRICT OF UTAH

Salt Lake City, Utah
September 1, 1943

Edward J. Ennis, Director
Alien Enemy Control Unit
Department of Justice
Washington, D.C

Dear Mr. Ennis:
Re: Midori Arthur Shimoda
D.J. File #146-13-2-77-254

I am advised by the Immigration and Naturalization Service representatives here that under an order of the Attorney General dated August 23, 1943, continuing in full force and effect, a previous order of parole dated May 4, 1943 concerning the above-named alien, who is presently detained at Missoula, Montana, has been vacated. I am further advised that this young man has been given an interimparole [*sic*] and this parole has been made dependent upon approval or disapproval by me. I think that I should disapprove this interim parole and am accordingly reporting to you the reason for this position.

This young man came to Utah at the time of the evacuation from California. He is a photographer by trade and an alien by birth. He apparently has had a good deal of educational opportunity and speaks the English language with real ease. When he came to Utah he did a peculiar thing to begin with. He left the rather populous portions of the state and went down into the southeast corner to the town of Monticello, where he was the only Japanese, and there engaged in his photographic operations. He had been there but a short time when he succeeded in making trouble for himself and he then moved from Monticello and went to Blanding, where he lived for a while, doing photographic work. He engratiated himself with some of the citizens there and appeared to be getting along all right, but an adverse report was made to the Federal Bureau of Investigations and that organization investigated him and he was arrested and brought to Salt Lake for hearing. The Enemy Alien Hearing Board heard his case and gave subject a chance to fully state his history, which he did in some detail. As the result of that hearing, he was paroled and was given opportunity for employment here in Salt Lake, which seemed to be very satisfactory to him. He was working for a photographer and continued in that line of work for five months. One day, with no apparent reason, Shimoda appeared before Inspector Mutz of the Immigration Bureau and told him that he had decided to quit his job and leave Salt Lake and that he was going to New York and that it didn't make any difference whether we would allow him to go or not, that he had determined to go and that he was impelled to take this step as the result of a confidential arrangement

*137*

which he had, and even though he knew that the result to him might be disastrous, he was going to go, with or without authority. Mr. Mutz tried to get a statement from alien as to what had determined him on this adventure and here he refused to talk and said that he planned to commit some act after leaving here, either with or without authority, which would eventually result in his internment. He was examined and re-examined upon the point and given an opportunity to be frank about what was worrying him. We could get absolutely nothing from him and so I concluded that a young man as bright as this alien was and as thoroughly equipped, might be dangerous running loose. Accordingly, I agreed with Mr. Mutz that he should be detained until our Enemy Alien Board could work on him. In the meantime an order came from Washington for internment at Missoula, Montana, so the hearing was never had.

As a result of my contacts with this man, I am convinced that he has a plan in mind to do something which may be harmful to the country or the people in it and have been thoroughly satisfied to have him interned, and for that reason I do not believe that he should be allowed on his own until we know more about what was impelling his wilful [*sic*] violation of orders and his determination to violate them, unless he was restrained. For that reason I am not in agreement with the parole order which has been recently made.

Very truly yours,
Dan B. Shields,
United States Attorney.
CC – Immigration and Naturalization Service Salt Lake City, Utah

## FORT MISSOULA

*Sometimes the picture will return, without the story.*[25]

The first time I went to the ruins of Japanese American incarceration, I found Midori's face. It was hanging on the wall of the barracks in Fort Missoula, Montana. Fort Missoula was the first incarceration site I was conscious of visiting. *Conscious*, because you cannot step foot anywhere in the United States without crossing a site where people have been targeted and detained. The fort was originally built to protect white settlers from the indigenous tribes—the Salish, as well as the Kootenai, Pend d'Oreille, Blackfeet, and Shoshone—who had lived in the valley for thousands of years. It was an open fort. There were no walls. The walls were assumed into the settlers' commitment to vigilance. In 1941, the Department of Justice transformed Fort Missoula into a prison. The prisoners were Italian and German nationals, and Japanese immigrants. The Issei were fifty-to-sixty-year-old men—religious leaders, teachers, business owners, gardeners, husbands, fathers, grandfathers—the majority of whom, propagandized as fifth column terrorists and classified as enemy aliens, had been detained in the days—hours,

---

25. Rea Tajiri, *History and Memory* (New York: Women Make Movies, 1991).

*139*

even—after the attack on Pearl Harbor. Midori was the youngest. He was in his early thirties.

Fort Missoula was not difficult to transform into a prison; it already possessed the qualities. In order for the settlers to be soothed by a sense of being protected, the fort had to establish the locus of power, cohesion, and sanctity on the inside. The outside—the landscape, its people—were, to the logic of the fort, illegible, dangerous. This was the land the settlers were occupying. White settlers were the original aliens. They sought to diffuse their alienation by claiming the land and controlling the movement and rights of the people for whom the land was not alien but ancestral. Fort Missoula did not need to be turned inside-out to become a prison. It only needed to reframe its identity.

It is now a historical museum. A hodgepodge of buildings and outbuildings—schoolhouse, carriage house, root cellar, church, train, tipi-burner, fire lookout, arranged across a field soft with prairie dog tunnels—that attempts to articulate the triumphal narrative of Manifest Destiny. It has the blinding quality of an abandoned amusement park. History collapsed into a single sprawling diorama. June, Susie, and Risa were the first in the family to return. They took pictures in front of the barracks, where a memorial stone had been planted.

I have a memory of June telling me, when I was young, that she visited Midori in Missoula. She was a teenager then, living with her family in the Elm Hotel in Salt Lake City. Midori lived down the hall. He was working for a photographer and was on parole. He was obligated to routinely check in with the Immigration Bureau, which was keeping track of his movements. Asano befriended Midori. They were close in age. Susie and Saburo and Teddy visited Midori in his apartment. He had a record collection. Susie remembers "The Donkey Serenade": *Though she may try to hide it / She cannot deny / There's a light in her eye / Oh the charm of her smile . . .*

Midori lived in the Elm for five months, until he told the Immigration Bureau that he was going to move, with or without their permission, to New York City. I remember June telling me that she and Susie, six years younger, rode the train to Missoula. Would two young Japanese American women have been allowed such freedom?

I asked June recently to tell me the story again. It had been awhile since I heard it. *I never went to Missoula*, she said.

She painted a summery picture. *He played baseball*, she said. Then added: *with the guards*. There was no scene without the guards. That Midori played baseball with the guards proclaimed the camaraderie of prison existence. That the war was *out there*, not circumscribed by the barbed wire fence, guns, the guard towers. *He went fishing with the guards*, June said. That Midori could stand side by side with a guard on the banks of the river, that he could sit side by side with a guard in the *Minnehaha*, the prisoners' boat, not only illustrated his exemplary character (kind, optimistic, resilient) and provided proof he was a model prisoner, but made me feel like I was being protected, lied to. And angry. I did not know at what: June for withholding from me the true story, or censoring it; Midori for withholding from June the true story, censoring it, or for standing side-by-side with the guards; or the guards. I imagined a field of blond dirt in a landscape so desolate and flat, the horizon, in every direction, was below the field of view. So flat, it curved. And a mass of men, in silhouette, compelled by an ambiguous hunger, an ultimatum, casting long shadows that expressed what remained of their spirit.

Censored from a letter Midori wrote from Fort Missoula to his sister-in-law, Hide Shimoda, in Springville, Utah, are the following nine words: *set up impresses me as a slave labor so.*[26]

The river is the Bitterroot, named after the flower, which grows white and pink and purple along the ground. I went to Fort Missoula for the first time in August 2004, when I moved to Missoula from North Carolina and had just arrived. The barracks were long, white, and removed from the rest of the museum, at the opposite end of the field. The building's abandonment reminded me of Dorothy's house being thrown down on the outskirts of Oz. Two small trees obscured the windows. The soil around the memorial stone was fresh, recently dug.

"FROM 1941 TO 1944, FORT MISSOULA SERVED AS A DETENTION CENTER FOR MORE THAN 1,000 ITALIANS, MORE THAN 1,000 JAPANESE, AND 22 GERMAN NATIONALISTS. THE ITALIANS WERE WORLD'S FAIR WORKERS AND CIVILIAN SEAMEN WHOSE SHIPS HAD BEEN IMPOUNDED AT THE OUTBREAK OF THE WAR IN EUROPE. THE JAPANESE WERE PROMINENT IN THEIR WEST COAST COMMUNITIES AND WERE CONSIDERED POTENTIALLY DANGEROUS. NONE OF EITHER GROUP WERE EVER CHARGED WITH BEING, OR PROVEN TO BE, ENEMY AGENTS.

THIS MEMORIAL IS DEDICATED TO THOSE MEN WHO WERE INTERNED AND HELD AT FORT MISSOULA WITHOUT TRIAL DURING WORLD WAR II. MAY THIS EVENT BE REMEMBERED."[27]

---

26. The censor was a Japanese American kibei named Paul Kashino, who worked as an interpreter for INS.
27. Quotation marks in the original.

Inside the barracks is the kind of starveling, patchwork exhibition you find in countless small-town museums across the country, in which any opportunity for critique is undone by hope, optimism. The building is one of the original barracks, yet I could sense neither the presence nor even the absence of the men. Their memory had been replaced by front pages of newspapers—*Honolulu Star-Bulletin*, December 7, 1941: *WAR! OAHU BOMBED BY JAPANESE PLANES*; *Seattle Post-Intelligencer*, December 8, 1941: *JAPAN, U.S. AT WAR*; again the *Post-Intelligencer*, April 13, 1945: *PRESIDENT IS DEAD!* The *Winona* (Minnesota) *Republican-Herald*, August 14, 1945: *JAPAN SURRENDERS! WORLD WAR OVER*—and dozens of photographs providing an idyllic narrative of incarceration: men in suits and hats eating noodles, men and women (although there were no female prisoners at Fort Missoula) on horses, men beside a boat, men performing judo in front of an audience of men, a man holding a trout, men at a funeral, a man crouching in strawberries, men on stage. The caption above the men on stage: *While Alien Hearing Boards were investigating the loyalties of the hapless Japanese, Immigration Service immigrant inspectors were busy interrogating many Japanese at Fort Missoula who they suspected were in the United States illegally.* Hapless, as if their incarceration was bad luck. The hearing board included INS and FBI agents, and interpreters, many of whom were Korean. The question was not the legality of the men being in the United States but their allegiance to it, the extent to which they had been drawn successfully away from Japan, their history, and, in no small part, themselves.

Three photographs stood out. In each, a man was wearing a light-colored dress, white gloves, stockings, high heels, and a wig of curly black hair. In one photograph he was holding a purse. In another he was lifting up his dress to expose his stockinged leg. A third photograph showed the man in a slip, sitting in front of a mirror. In two of the photographs he was surrounded by other men, all in suits and ties. He was the only man, in all the photographs on the walls, in a dress, therefore, to my mind, in disguise.

I went to the ruins expecting to see Midori's face, but I did not think I would see Midori's face, so when I saw Midori's face, I felt sick. It was the kind of uncanny recognition that registers first as nausea. I turned away. Then turned back, leaned closer, and touched him. The wall fell back. The roof of the barracks lifted off. Midori's face was brighter than daylight. And though I remember it being warm and round and full of love—I was a part of it—I remember it being gray and soft and unaccountably sad, of a sadness I could not name. I saw my father's face, for the first time, in the frame of incarceration. I saw Kelly's face. The sun had fallen to earth, revealing its exact size and dimension.

Who has the nerve to touch the sun?

Midori was staring through the mirror. Through the photographer. Through the guards. Through the mountains surrounding the valley. Through the clouds washing down the faces of the mountains. I felt like I was being thrown, through Midori's face, into the immediacy of a history that was, until then, remote, more or less extinct.

I ran across the field. The only person in the museum was the woman in the gift shop, Sharon. I told her I had just come from the barracks, that Midori was hanging on the wall. I described him. Out of breath. She told me to wait a minute then disappeared. She returned with a three-ring binder and an envelope. The binder contained photographs of the prisoners, mostly Italian, a few Germans, some Japanese. The Italians called Missoula *Bella Vista*. They were from Europe, lived in Europe. They were not immigrants. Some of them stayed in the valley after their release, so beautiful was their view. The photographs depicted the interstitial, less photogenic moments that illuminated incarceration as wasteland, arbitrary, confusion. The envelope contained five photographs from the binder Sharon had photocopied. All five were of Midori. They were taken by Peter Fortune, an INS agent in Hawaii, called up to Fort Missoula, where he worked in food service and, in his free time, took photographs.[28] In one of the photographs, Midori is wearing a bra and white slip, skin-toned stockings rolled down his thighs, and black shoes and is posing alone, smiling.

Midori's body and face are a map describing a territory I

---

28. Fortune spent time in Okinawa after the war, before moving to Washington State. An oil painting he exhibited at the Frye Museum in Seattle was titled *A Grandson Rises* (1962).

know, think I know, or have known, but which looks, from the vantage of this graphic projection of him, unfamiliar, another territory altogether. I try to locate myself. Every landmark and place name, every feature, is visible, if not accessible, at once, but the cardinal directions have switched places, gone missing.

I have always associated hair that stands straight up off a person's head as evidence of the restlessness of their thoughts. Midori's ears are large. When I squint, his ears move. His right leg is up on a wooden bench. His right hand is cupping his knee. His left leg is bent. The back of his left hand, pressed against his hip, covered by the waistline of the slip, hanging mid-thigh, evokes restraint. Two veins run the length of his left forearm. The vein in his right arm, corresponding to the vein on the underside of his left, is visible, originating in the terminal of his elbow, snaking to his wrist. That is where I see myself most clearly. In his veins. And arms. His right arm straight, partially obscured, at his bicep, by his bra and chest. His left pectoral visible between his shoulder and the top of the bra. Two eels are swimming beneath his skin. His stockings are rolled down his thighs just below the hem of the slip. The slip is tight, though soft. The waistline of his slip is folded in above his navel. The hem of his slip is a fringe of wide circles. Around each circle is a wider circle. A black line beginning at the top of his right thigh swoops at his crotch. The line tapers, disappears, into whiteness.

Midori's eyes are clear, almost wet, with the flash of the bulb twice-reflected. His eyebrows are slightly raised. It is there that I begin to sense skepticism, concern. Distrust, and its corresponding lack of agency. Resignation. Two lines on his forehead form a pediment. He is smiling, but the lines around his eyes are unmoved. His upper lip is straight, unconvinced. Sometimes his smile is a wave. Sometimes a wound. Sometimes not entirely his. If not, to whom (how many people, entities, institutions) does it belong?

Midori did not know Peter Fortune. Nor did he know who would see this photograph. He posed in several dimensions at once. Half-naked, proud, even triumphant, he is, against a wall of thick timber, performing. But the longer I stare at his body and face—his eyes and his smile—the less convinced I become that he is actually sharing, or free to share, any part of himself. Who he is, and what he is feeling, is being sublimated, suppressed, by his outward appearance, pushed down the deep well of his throat, into his chest, but beyond the reach of his heart.

When I left the museum—the barracks, the fields—I felt infused with the spirit of connection. Midori and I had been reunited! But the feeling did not last. There was no sense that Midori had been waiting. For me, his grandson, anyone. Almost as soon as the *body* and *face* of incarceration were revealed, they were replaced with an unconquerable loneliness. The sky was low and tyrannically white. The mountains, in the distance, were suddenly very close, cliff-like and impenetrable. I called June, then my father. Their voices were soft, underwater. It was not that they did not seem interested in the photographs, but they did not ask any questions, which caused me to doubt what I had seen. It was true: the barracks, isolated and staged, manifested an alternate universe, one in which my desperation had been appeased. I had reduced the history of incarceration not only to Midori's face, but to my desire to understand.

I slept for one year with Fortune's photograph of Midori. Under my pillow, sometimes under my body. I wanted to sink with Midori through the bed, through the floor, into the ground, to commingle with what of him had been arrested.

At night, Midori slipped out of bed. I woke to see him climbing the wall. I watched him rise up the wall and curve onto the ceiling. I watched him slide down the wall and curve onto the floor.

The moment Midori touched the floor, two voices emerged: the voice of a young woman and the voice of an old man. The voices emerged from behind my right ear, as if out of my shoulder. The woman and the man were talking to each other. Their voices were clear, I could hear every word. Sometimes they talked about me, and though I wondered what they made of me, I never discerned any judgment, only a kind of subtle expectation. I wondered if the young woman and the old man were related. I had the feeling they were the same person, in two different phases of being: the young woman at the furthest limit of herself as an immigrant before becoming a citizen, the old man at the furthest limit of himself as a citizen before becoming a corpse. I tried, every night, to write down what they were saying, but whenever I shifted, or fell further into sleep, their voices became softer, blurred together, then dissolved. Only shadows, rising and falling.

I refer to this photograph as Midori's grave, because it is an icon of his arrest and was the first, most accessible place I could go to visit him after death. It is ironic, fitting, and utterly infuriating that his grave revealed itself to me on the wall of the barracks in which he was held under the pretext of being a threat to the national security of the country of which I am a citizen.

On September 11, 1942, while being interrogated by the FBI, Midori said he thought Japan was hell. *Japan is hell,* he said. *I don't want to go back.* But then he said: *I wish they would give me a gun to go and fight Japan.*

Midori was not born an enemy alien. He was made into an enemy alien. The first (alien) phase was immigration. The third (enemy) phase was the attack on Pearl Harbor. The second phase was the transition. Which was, for a Japanese man, ineligible for citizenship, compulsory. The United States was a series of circles, administered by laws and acts, through which people rose and fell. If Midori betrayed any suggestion of love for Japan, he would have been plunged down the circles, and if he had not pledged his allegiance to the United States, he would have been deported. Self-hatred, momentary or enduring, locates hell in the birthplace of the self. Midori was trying to escape.

What did he mean when he said *Japan is hell*? Did he mean the Hell of Repetition? Did he mean the Hell of the Black Rope? Did he mean the Hell of All Living Beings? Did he mean the Hell of Lamentations, the Hell of Great Lamentations? Did he mean the Hell of Scorching Heat, the Hell of Great Scorching Heat? Did he mean the Hell of No-Interval? Did he mean the Hell of Black Threads, the Hell of Great Screaming? Did he mean the Hell of Great Burning? Did he mean the Hell of Perpetual Suffering? Did he mean the Hell of Black Sand Clouds, of Shit, of Five Spikes, the Hell of Starvation? Did he mean the Hell of Blinding Thirst, of Blood and Pus, of Boiling Pot, of Many Boiling Pots? Did he mean the River of Ash, the Hell of Ice, of Forgetting? Or, because it was invoked in a moment in which he was trapped and without choice, a hell even more desperate? I think of the crimes the Imperial Japanese Army was committing throughout Asia. I think of the crimes Japan was committing against its own people. I think of the crimes the United States was committing against both Japan and its own people. The situation that produced such a denunciation of the self was not one but an infinite number of hells. These are the multifarious flames illuminating Midori's smile.

The prisoners at Fort Missoula put on plays. Other prisoners, the guards, the staff, even townspeople were invited to attend. One of the plays, allegedly, was *Madame Butterfly*, a play set in Nagasaki, though more universally in the colonial imagination. If true, it would be terribly symbolic, given that *Madame Butterfly* is a story of dehumanization, exploitation, and theft, masquerading as a fantasy of sacrifice and allegiance.

Madame Butterfly, a fifteen year-old Japanese girl, has traditionally been played by white actors. The first actor to ever play Madame Butterfly was Italian. The second was Ukrainian. The first to play Madame Butterfly in the United States was Hungarian, followed by a white American. It was not that white women were appropriating the character of a Japanese girl. White women invented her. They invented her so as to have not only a body but an effigy through which to sing. The story, in which a Japanese girl is invented by whiteness in order to be exploited, then eventually killed, and under the pretense of love, places it firmly within the same tradition that produced Japanese American incarceration.

A young U.S. Navy lieutenant falls in love with a Japanese girl named Cho-Cho (Madame Butterfly). The lieutenant asks Cho-Cho to marry him. She says yes. She converts to Christianity. When her family finds out, they denounce the marriage and disown Cho-Cho, which strengthens the bond between her and the lieutenant. They marry. Immediately after, the lieutenant leaves for three years. Cho-Cho dutifully waits. One day a letter arrives: The lieutenant has married an American woman. Cho-Cho writes back: *But I've given birth to your child, you have to come back, I would rather die than be abandoned.* The lieutenant returns, but with the American woman. They have come to take Cho-Cho's son. Cho-Cho never sees the lieutenant, but meets the American woman and reluctantly surrenders her son. She gives her son—her half-white American, half-Japanese son—a U.S. flag, then takes a knife and slashes her throat.

Her choice was familiar to anyone whose acceptance as an equal member of white western society is provisional, whose existence is, in part, the invention of that same heedless society. It is not a choice. The blood that spills is an emanation of western desire—the desire to have and behold, and ultimately behead, that which it fears and willfully fails to understand.

One summer, Kelly joined Spotlight Theater, a small, bedraggled group of aspiring actors who put on plays on a small stage in the parking lot of a retirement community in Ridgefield, Connecticut, where we grew up. They put on a production of *South Pacific*. Kelly played Liat, the young Tonkinese girl. Liat falls in love with a US Marine lieutenant. She lives with her mother, Bloody Mary, on the island of Bali-ha'i. Bloody Mary tries to arrange a marriage between her daughter and the lieutenant. The lieutenant ultimately declines Bloody Mary's proposal. His family back home disapproves of him marrying an Asian woman. Plus, she is a teenager, but that is somehow irrelevant.

Bali-ha'i is a nonexistent volcano. Kelly wore makeup around her eyes that made her eyes look narrower. She did not speak. She had no lines. Her role consisted of smiling and staring longingly at the lieutenant.

*I was really excited to get the lead. That was back when I thought I would be an actress and I thought I was really good or must be really good when I got that part. I remember it was kind of a steamy role. I had to wear a sarong and cuddle up to the director's son or grandson, I forget who he was. I later realized I probably only got it because I was the only Asian looking person around. I think my looks were the reason for lots of things growing up.*[29]

---

29. Kelly Shimoda, in an email, June 26, 2013.

There were a little over 20,000 people living in Ridgefield at the time. Two percent were Asian. The stage lights were hot and poorly aimed. Kelly squinted through her makeup. Her smile was a grimace. If she was acting at all, it was a betrayal of her character's frustration at being caught between the manipulations of her mother and the cowardice of the man she was supposed to love.

I lived in Missoula for four years. I left in the spring of 2008. It rained for one month. The rivers flooded. A tree growing on the bank of the river where I was living lost its grip and fell into the water. I heard the roots tearing out of the earth. The tree fell slowly, formed a slash in the air.

## DREAMS

A monk is sitting behind me. I can feel his smirk on the back of my neck. The secret of the monk's success: he believes in nothing. Everything is. There is no need for belief. But the monk's lack of belief is specific. He devised a way to understand life and called it *suffering*. But the monk is intolerant. He cannot bear the sight of his demented grandparents vomiting. They will be dead soon. Their deaths will open a gap in which will materialize a vision of the monk's immortal self.

The monk saw his grandparents naked once, curled up in a bed that resembled an enormous nest, made of sticks, hair, newspapers. He had never seen them naked before and was struck by how indistinguishable their bodies were—gray, flaccid—from one another. *Life is already too long*, he thought. He wanted his grandparents to be young again. It looked very much like the fruits of suffering: speechlessness, incontinence, loss of faculties, an age-old bitterness, fermented.

I explain to my cello teacher that I am having trouble playing with emotion. *It's stuck behind the fingerboard*, I say. He takes the cello and turns it around, then tells me to try again.

A truck pulls into the parking lot behind the building where I am struggling with the cello. The truck is mud-brown and green. In its trailer lives a troupe of kabuki actors. The trailer has ventilation slits that cannot be seen from the outside. When the moment is right, the top and sides of the trailer are taken down to form a stage, and the actors are revealed, but when is the moment right? There is only one moment, and it must be summoned: if someone asks the driver, *What's in the trailer?* But no one ever asks. The kabuki actors stay in the trailer, keeping themselves occupied, justifying their imprisonment by saying to themselves that they are rehearsing, always rehearsing.

Kabuki used to be performed only by men. That has changed. The women, who have replaced the men, resent the question. They are not content to perform for anyone who asks. That criterion, no matter how infrequently invoked, is, they feel, completely lacking in the respect with which a stranger must ask after what they do not yet know is magic. The women would prefer to rehearse in the privacy of their trailer—in the blades of light stretching through the ventilation slits. Unlike the men, their imaginations do not depend upon the walls. Their rehearsing is devotional. They would prefer to create their performance as a permanently foreign language.

The best time to see a performance is in the winter, just after it snows. It is then that the actors' costumes, composed of every shape and color, seem, against the surrounding white, to float, electrified.

## NEW YORK CITY

Midori sang a song about pigeons. In the afternoons, at night, putting us to bed. I can still hear the beginning:

> *Hato-poppo, hato-poppo, poppo poppo . . .*
> *Poppo pigeons, poppo pigeons, poppo poppo, come down*
> *    from the temple roof.*
> *Don't leave, poppo poppo, stay here and play with me.*

It is the only memory I have of my grandfather's voice.

The first time Midori and June had sex, Midori cried. This is the story I was told. It was my introduction to sex: two old people reimagined as young people, naked and crying. They were in a hotel room on 86th Street between First and Second Avenues. June was in her late teens. Midori was in his thirties. It was 1944. Their age difference was mentioned but never discussed. Soon enough, to my young mind, they were old, the differences in their ages erased. Then the differences in their ages became hereditary, tradition, a modern permutation of the differences in the ages between the picture brides and the men they did not know. The story was that Midori cried because he was relieved June was a virgin, which mattered, to him, because the story behind that story was that three years earlier he had walked in on his first wife with another man. Why was it important to share with children, grandchildren, the image—the ambience—of their grandmother as a virgin? The image of Midori opening the door on his first wife forced me to close the door and open it again on my grandparents, naked and crying. The story was supposed to be sweet. I heard the story, over time, however, as the possessiveness of a man who, with his face contorted, did not resemble my dying grandfather, and as the justification for closing the door, or wanting to, on the past, in favor of the future, of innocence.

*I remember looking out the window and watching Cleveland in lights*, June wrote about the train ride from Salt Lake to New York City. Midori was waiting on the platform at Grand Central. *We figured it was destiny*, she said. She and Midori had been writing letters. It was the only writing of his she could remember. Their letters disappeared. She remembers leaving Grand Central and walking toward Fifth Avenue, looking up at the buildings and thinking to herself, *I'm a hick*.

Midori arrived a year earlier, in the winter. He had two small duffle bags and Setsuo's overcoat. He stayed at the YMCA on 63rd and Central Park West. He found a job in the Carnegie Hall building retouching photos for a German couple, then for a photography studio on West 47th Street near Fifth Avenue. During the interview, the photographer, Robert Keene, told Midori that his roommate in college was Japanese; he wondered what happened to him. He hired Midori but said that if any of his customers complained, he would have to let him go.

Midori and June were engaged December 14, 1944. *It was the last time I got drunk*, June said. They celebrated with their friends Vivian and Martin at a nightclub. Hazel Scott sang. Jimmy Savo performed. Vivian was food editor at *Redbook*. She hired

Midori as a photographer. She also hired June—as a house-keeper. *Between helping with chores, I taste-tested Vivian's food*, June wrote. *She stayed thin; I got chubby. To make a few dollars I helped Vivian with sewing.*

*Vivian asked me if I would help her fix and clean the brown-stone they bought in exchange for room and board. The brownstone had been empty a long time; it had been owned by the Ruppert (beer) fam-ily. This was 93rd Street between Second and Third Ave. The second floor was a living room that opened onto a dining room. Outside the dining room was a butler's pantry where they keep the good dishes. The food was brought in on a dumb waiter. Vivian and Martin's bedroom was on the third floor. I was in a small room.*

The wedding was January 15, 1945, at Vivian's. It was snowing. Midori and June had little money. Vivian paid for everything. She set up an altar in her dining room. June's dress came from a wholesale warehouse. They bought rings in Chinatown. Kenji Nogaki, who worked at Bloomingdale's on 59th Street, brought flowers. Aiko Tashiro played the piano. A Japanese Methodist minister officiated.

Asano arrived by bus. Her luggage was lost, so she bor-rowed one of Vivian's dresses. John and Rae Yasumura and their daughter Eileen, who later died of leukemia, were there. Mrs. Yagi and her daughter and husband. Tubby. The four Hawaiian boys Midori and June met at Miyako Restaurant. Vivian's brothers Bert and Manny, his wife Cecile, their son Mark. Mr. and Mrs. Shup. Midori's friend Minoru Yamasaki was there. Everyone called him Tinky. He and Midori grew up togeth-er in Seattle. Tinky, Kenji Nogaki, George *Porgy* Okada, June Okazaki, Clarence Arai, Taft Beppu (and his brothers Lincoln and Grant), Aiko Tashiro. *I wish I could remember more of them*, June said.

1926

Tinky was living in New York when Midori arrived. He helped Midori find an apartment in the building where he was living, on the corner of 87th and First Avenue. The building overlooked the Hell Gate strait of the East River, home to the black-crowned night heron, and the site of the largest planned explosion prior to the testing of the atomic bomb. On October 10, 1885, the Army Corps of Engineers detonated 300,000 pounds of explosives to blast the rocks and reefs that had sunk hundreds of ships.

Tinky designed the World Trade Center. The centerpieces were the two 110-story towers. He planned each to be 80 stories but, to satisfy an arcane city ordinance, added 30 stories. The North Tower was completed December 23, 1970. The South Tower was completed July 19, 1971. The complex was officially opened April 4, 1973. Tinky spoke at the opening. *The World Trade Center*, he said, *is a living symbol of man's dedication to world peace, a representation of man's belief in humanity, his need for individual dignity, his beliefs in the cooperation of men, and, through cooperation, his ability to find greatness.*[30]

---

30. Minoru Yamasaki, April 4, 1973.

The first thing I did when I woke up was write down my dream. From my journal, September 11, 2001: *There's a rock on a lake. A rope hangs from the branch of an old tree over the water. The rope's reflection in the water resembles a snake struggling to climb down its own body. Wind is rising off the water. The rope is swinging. People are climbing the rock and swinging on the rope into the lake. The lake is black except where the bodies are landing beneath the swinging rope where it's green. The sun is touching the lake, withdrawing light from the surface.*

To climb down or escape its own body. I stepped out of my apartment in Brooklyn and looked west. A column of smoke was drifting over Manhattan. Apartment building on fire, I thought I would read later. When the first airplane flew into the North Tower, I was on the L-train, beneath the East River, reading Haruki Murakami's *Underground*, about how, in March 1995, the religious cult Aum Shinrikyo released sarin gas in the Tokyo subway, killing thirteen and injuring thousands. *Two planes have crashed into the World Trade Center*, a man said to the woman next to him. When I emerged from the subway onto Lexington Avenue, everyone was on a cell phone or everyone's cell phone was ringing.

*You Americans are so sensitive*, a French woman said. I had been standing in the middle of Madison Avenue, facing south, watching smoke rising off the end of the city, and had just gone back into the bookstore where I worked. We were closing early, the city was under indeterminate siege, had fallen into a disorder that was, in that moment of unknowing, as exhilarating as it was terrifying, when a French couple asked if I would help them find a book of paintings by Courbet. *I'm sorry, we're closing*, I said, although I did not say *I'm sorry*. What did we know? Two airplanes had flown into each of the Twin Towers, and one of the towers had fallen. We knew, before that, that it was a scenario that every one of us had dreamed. That is when the woman said, *You Americans are so sensitive.*

I walked ninety blocks from the bookstore to my friend's apartment in the East Village where people were gathering to watch the news and make or try to make phone calls and sit on the roof and watch the smoke. Everyone was in the streets. Then the streets were empty. W. H. Auden's *unmentionable odour of death / Offends the September night* was quoted.[31] People began to remember, even as what they were remembering was happening. Candlelight vigils grew out of the shaken ground, spreading seas of flame and flowers and wax, and, for a few days, a loving solidarity was genuine among the people. But just as quickly, the police, empowered by their election to the status of heroes, imposed their force and, in the name of order and safety, broke up the gatherings, swept the parks and sidewalks and streets clean of demonstrations of peace. Auden continued revising his poem after publication, changing the line *We must love one another or die* to *We must love one another and die.* Lyndon Johnson used the line in a television ad for his 1964 presidential campaign, in which the image of a young girl picking petals from a daisy transitions into the image of an atomic bomb explosion.

*My experience of him doing photography at the studio and at home (like when we got up at dawn to sit by a flower waiting for the sun to hit the dew on a petal as a bumblebee arrived for breakfast)—it meant sitting still for minutes, and minutes, and minutes. . . .*[32]

---

31. W. H. Auden, September 1, 1939.

32. Risa Shimoda, in an email, January 30, 2011.

Midori set up his tripod and camera in the grass not far from the flower but far enough so the flower would not be self-conscious. Bees approached the flower, some landed on it. Midori rose many times to the viewfinder. When the flower was alone, Midori was attracted to it yet felt it was too unknowable. When a bee approached the flower and landed on it, he was captivated by the bee but felt it dispossessed the flower of a mystery that elevated both to a kind of ecstatic sympathy. It was only in the moment immediately before the bee landed on the flower that Midori felt a sense of immortality.

For years after the end of the war, Midori continued to be visited by FBI agents inquiring about his work, looking through his contact sheets, negatives. Their visits to his studio on the southwest corner of Bryant Park and Sixth Avenue became commonplace. I hoped, hearing this story, that he was hiding something from the FBI—something subversive, a record, for example, of the enfeeblement of the United States in the form of FBI functionaries belaboring the racism of the state through transparently pointless visitations.

A private elevator connected a narrow side entrance to Midori's studio. The most striking feature of his studio was the enormous fireplace, its hearth, tall enough to stand in, resembling the open doorway of a small cathedral.

The first time Midori visited the studio, a red couch was suspended from the ceiling above the fireplace. It looked like a carcass. The studio, and the building, had once belonged to William Randolph Hearst. Hearst built the studio, formerly an apartment, with separate entrance and elevator and enormous fireplace, for his mistress.

## AFRICAN BURIAL GROUND

It had started raining by the time I reached the African burial ground in lower Manhattan. The wind was blowing white flower petals onto the seven grass-covered mounds. A black man was leading a tour of white boy scouts. The scouts, not yet teenagers, were huddled in a half-circle. They wore blue short-sleeve button-down shirts with yellow neckerchiefs and khaki shorts. The tour guide was explaining the burial ground's most conspicuous feature: a granite chamber, twenty-five feet tall: The Door of Return. It jutted upward from the ground like the bridge of a submarine or the fin of a monstrous shark. The Door of Return he said, was the inverse of the Door of No Return on Gorée Island, off the coast of Senegal, in Elmina Castle, on the coast of Ghana, up and down the west coast of Africa. *It was through that door*, the tour guide said, raising his voice above the wind and rain, *that the African slaves were* . . . then he stopped, mid-sentence, and hesitated, before finding the word he must have determined, in that moment, to be the least upsetting for his audience: *relocated*. I noticed his right eye. It was white, completely opaque. The boy scouts were silent, obliging.

From 1712 until 1794, approximately 15,000 Africans, free and enslaved, were buried in a 6.6-acre plot of land just beyond the northern border of (then) New Amsterdam. The first burials likely predated 1712. An earlier burial ground, open to all, was taken over in 1697 by Trinity Church. Their resolution stated: *no person or Negro whatsoever, do presume to break up any ground for the burying of his Negro, as they will answer it at their peril.* African burials were forced to the outskirts of the city, to the shore of a small pond. Half of the 15,000 burials were children.

The burial ground closed in 1794. Over the next two hundred years, the graveyard was buried beneath twenty-five feet of development. In 1991, the graves were discovered during the initial phase of the construction of a federal building. The remains of 419 Africans were exhumed, wrapped in shrouds, placed in coffins, and reburied in seven mounds, which were dedicated in 1993. The mounds were covered in grass. Flowering trees were planted. The graves of the other approximately 14,580 Africans remained, untouched, for the most part undiscovered, underground.

If we marked every death—not even yet a grave—with a mound, the earth would be covered in mounds. The mounds would act as impassive prophecy, to which the living grow accustomed, in understanding their bodies, their destinies, death, in general, as being part of the evolving topography of earth.

The African burial ground is now a memorial to the African burial ground. The plot has been reduced to 0.34 acres. A graveyard of a graveyard. The other 6.26 acres have been devoured—by the NYPD across Elk, U.S. Citizenship and Immigration Services and the U.S. Court of International Trade across Duane Street, and the IRS next door.

Ten minutes away, on foot, are two enormous (one acre) square holes (cubes), each three times the size of the African burial ground, cut deep into the ground. Water cascades down the walls into pools. In the center of each pool are smaller square holes, into which the pools overflow. The water falls, or slides—snakes—down the walls of these smaller holes. The holes mark the footprints of the Twin Towers. They, the twin holes, are meant to memorialize September 11, 2001.

When I stood at the parapet, inscribed with the names of the dead, the evanescent, snake-like gestures of the water down the walls resembled smoke. The bottoms of the holes cannot be seen. Only if you were standing at the window in one of the surrounding buildings, or flying, would you be able to see the bottom. The fact of whether or not there is a bottom, or bottomlessness, is a matter of faith. Like peering into a well at night.

A young white girl, eleven or twelve, was posing in a black tutu beneath a slender white oak. An older white woman was taking her picture. Tourists started taking the young girl's picture. The young ballerina was as much a part of the spectacle as the holes. As were the tourists, taking pictures. The tableaux could have been replicated, a hall of mirrors, forever.

It was a weekday afternoon in spring. The rain and wind had let up. Puddles covered the plaza. There were thousands of tourists, from all over the world, but the plaza did not feel like an international place. It did not feel like a mixing of cultures. Not utopic. Not communal. No one seemed to know exactly where, or at what, to look. People's facial expressions were glazed, overawed, the faces of people wandering in place while inhabiting, or haunting, the aspect and attitude of contemplation.

Are people meant to contemplate the holes as if they are graves? Graves without bodies? Are the holes then ritual (as opposed to burial) graves? Do they symbolize the evacuation of bodies? Or are the holes themselves the evacuation of bodies?

Have the bodies been deprived of their graves, deprived of their corpses, even?

The holes are not referred to as *holes*. They are referred to as *pools*. And the memorial has a title, *Reflecting Absence*, which assumes its visitors into its meaning. That visitors will embody the memorial's meaning by reflecting on what has been lost. Which is precisely the aspect and attitude of their glazed, over-awed contemplation.

And yet, the memorial seems too conceptual to satisfy the patriotism stirred by—and maintained since—September 11, 2001. I was surprised, at least, that I did not sense the exertions of nationalistic yearning. I felt instead (or in addition), the overabundance of dispassionate eyes. People had assumed, as if by right of world citizenship, the responsibility, whether by reflex or indoctrination, of surveillance. Everyone looked like they were watching everyone else, fearing or fantasizing (what is the difference?) an assailant, a terrorist, while being watched over by the horrid compensation of the tallest building in the hemisphere, One World Trade Center.

Does the memorial preach? Despite the confidence of its spectacle, its message is unclear. Unsettled. It wants to say more, maybe even more darkly. The people, unsure of what it is they are supposed to be contemplating, hold it to a false and impossible ideal. To memorialize catastrophe and trauma. To memorialize the ongoing abstraction of death formalized by September 11, 2001, which made death, in the American imagination, rapturous.

And a source of pride. People took—continue to take—pride in the fact that many ethnicities were represented among the dead, as if the United States is only able to realize its democratic ambitions by being attacked. To memorialize, then, democracy, or democratic ambition, as a chimera that appears only in the emanations rising off the embers of death.

A true descent, following the water down into the memorial holes, would carry one back to the African burial ground. Where the pretense of the holes' concern is exposed, and can be visited, and where the betrayal of enigmatic pride resides.

On any given day, thousands of people tour the twin holes. They can trace, with their fingers, as well as their minds, the names of the dead. On any given day, a handful of people, many whom are passersby, visit the African burial ground. There are no names to trace. The dead have been commingled. And made permanently other. A 1731 law limited the number of Africans who could gather for a funeral to twelve. Grieving was outlawed. The law sought to separate the living from the dead. Death had to become fugitive. Not only were the lives of the Africans constrained, if not entirely circumscribed, by whites, but so were their deaths.

The secret life of memorials is not as much a secret as a subtext: that the memorial will not only outlast the people who might remember, who might have experienced, what is being memorialized, but people in general: human beings, entirely. That is what I see when I see seven mounds or twin holes in the ground (or, for that matter, memorial statues, plaques, signposts, inscriptions, etc.): a future in which only memorials remain. Then the future will be the memorial. To all that came before. The mounds and the holes will endure as enigmatic earthworks, expressing, exerting their language, their code, for no audience, but for the people-less earth.

The fugitive sense has not been relinquished. To stand in—not to pass—what remains of the African burial ground, surrounded by the scar tissue of Lower Manhattan, feels fugitive, because it feels like you are being surveilled, tabulated. Because of the scar tissue, in the form of the surrounding buildings with their thousands of windows, and the people who manufacture the blood of their businesses, loom, and are watching. And because it feels like you are standing against the current, in a surreptitious, subliminal hole.

When I returned to the African burial ground, the white petals on the seven grass-covered mounds had formed, in the hole and on the eyes of the dead, an ephemeral yet even more bottomless sky.

## THUNDER HILL

*For forty-nine days we seek to bring the dead*
*to awareness; it is words again that lead them astray.*[33]

A circular light hangs low in the sky. A wall grows out of the
ground. The light is pale yellow and white. The wall grows up
to meet it. There is little movement, except for the growing of
the wall and the perimeter of the light, restive, expectant. It is a
perfect, changeless circle—an illuminated lens, small white sun.

My father used to tell us this story. He told it to his cousins, a brother and sister, when they were young, then to Kelly
and me. He first told us in our front yard. I remember the trees:
a row of tulip trees, then gray birch, thousands, interminable.
The trees formed a wall, and I remember a circular light, shining beyond the furthest birch, yet seeming to hover in front of
it. I remember a white sky and not a thing overhead.

Two children, a boy and a girl, are standing in the yard of their
house, facing the woods. The woods go on without end. The
children notice, in the woods, something glowing, circular, like
a small white sun, a little more than halfway up from the ground
to the tops of the trees. The small white sun is silent, tantalizing.

---

33. Tsering Wangmo Dhompa, *My Rice Tastes Like the Lake* (Berkeley,
CA: Apogee Press, 2011).

The children enter the woods. The light, a perfect, change-less circle, appears to swing, but is still.

The children walk through the tulip trees into the birches. The ground is covered with leaves; the children are surrounded by the birches. They do not turn around. They never look back.

The birches are all the same width and height. The children do not touch them. They walk faster. The birches approach and vanish in the sound of the leaves. The light does not grow, nor do the children seem to be getting closer to it, though they are now running, the birches streaking past. The boy and the girl are running, running through the woods. The light hangs yellow and pale.

As the children run, a stone wall rises from the ground among the birches in the distance. The wall appears, grows bigger. The distance expands then collapses. The children see it, the wall; they are running, getting closer. They come to it, cannot stop, so together jump over the wall.

The circular light hangs in the white sky.


I have a recurring dream. I am in a house on a hill. From outside, the house appears small. Inside, it goes on forever. I open doors and find additional rooms, each room with additional doors. Most of the rooms are dark and small, with low ceilings, though others are large, light coming in through curtained windows. I keep finding doors to hidden rooms and narrow wooden stair-wells tucked behind walls that lead to additional floors.

I told this dream to my mother and she said, *I have the same dream!*


*I've just bought a rambling multistory house. The house is old, thick molding, heavily paneled doors. Some rooms are dark and small, others are large and light. I find hidden rooms. Hidden wings or floors. I might be walking down a hallway with rooms on either side, doors open, sunlight through the windows to the floor (wooden), and at the end of the hallway is a door. I open it to a large room, like a ballroom. Or I open it to a staircase that leads to other rooms. Sometimes these rooms are occupied by former tenants. Maybe I know I'm not allowed to trespass into these spaces.*

*There's usually a feeling of delight in finding rooms I didn't know about. It might be I discover a nice large bathroom with an old-fashioned tub and black and white tile floors with pale blue or green walls and white trim and that on the other side of that bathroom is a door to more rooms. It seems the only way to enter some of the rooms is through other rooms or through closets or lost stairwells. I'm most delighted when I discover an entire floor or a large attic. I don't recall seeing furniture. My attention is on the architectural features, the molding, floors, wall colors or paneling, windows large and small, staircases, any light that comes through the windows.*[34]

We enter the rooms of our lives and find them empty. We dream a life into the rooms, and, with the effects of our dreams, the rooms become ours. We enter and set about making our lives a reflection of life outside the rooms. Where we insist on solace and solitude, we adorn the room with the faces of people we know and love or claim to know and love but never actually see. Our rooms become installations of mirrors arranged to show the way we want to see ourselves, a synthesis of the ways we imagine the world outside to be when we are not in it. Our internal selves do not recognize our external selves, waving, on the surface—flags sequined by sixteen winds—while the external world, expanding at the mercy of disjointed souls, accreting and widening beyond self and perception, races away, insensate and indistinguishable from the limitlessness of space.

I wonder about an empty room: is it dilating or contract-

---

34. Karen McAlister Shimoda, in an email, June 8, 2013.

ing? With nothing inside, I have less by which to measure. For a room in which objects have been arranged, the confusion deepens. It becomes an irreversible lie. The room is dilating and contracting, but the objects in the room are forcing the illusion of motionlessness, in which everything is frozen in anticipation of the entrance of a being to assure us it is, at last, alright, okay, okay, it is alright to breathe.

I am sitting in a chair in the corner of the family room of the house where I grew up, 26 Thunder Hill Lane, Ridgefield, Connecticut. The room is small. Dark, but warm. The walls are wood paneling. To my right is a small, dark-green, wood-burning stove.

Midori enters. He sits in an orange and white wing-back chair opposite me. I am shocked by his presence. I tell him, nervously, that I have been writing a book about him. It is called *The Grave on the Wall*. I have already embarrassed myself. Then I ask how is he doing. He answers in Japanese, but I cannot hear him. I am disarmed by his presence. I ask another question but cannot hear myself. He answers in English this time. Is he looking at me? I stare at the moles on his cheeks. His nose is crooked. His eyebrows are short, full and gray. His mouth is closed in a straight line. His ears are long. His white-gray hair is parted on the left. He is wearing a sweater with a collared shirt. He is in his seventies, the age I remember him.

Then we are at a table. Light is coming through a sliding glass door hung with blood-red curtains. I want to show him things I have collected about his life—photographs of him, by him, his FBI file. Everything feels miscellaneous, misguided, pathetic. Also: presumptuous and intrusive, as if I have assumed the role of the FBI. I show him a photograph taken when he was incarcerated at Fort Missoula, in which he is wearing a bra, slip and stockings, and is smiling directly into the camera.

He recognizes the moment, though he has never seen the photograph.

*I told them No three times*, he says.

The curtains move slightly. I show Midori a photograph of him in the Chinzan-so garden in Tokyo. The House of Camellia. The pagoda is one thousand years old. It was transferred to Tokyo from the mountains outside Hiroshima. He has never seen the photograph. Then I show him surveillance photographs of mining and industrial sites taken with telephoto lenses from the roofs of small, abandoned buildings, the tops of ridges, behind rocks. Photographs of indeterminate desert landscapes. Midori is patient and looks at whatever I set before him without betraying any emotion, as if to say,

*No, this is not me. None of this is me.*

庭は夏の日ざかりの日を浴びて.

Midori threatened to kill himself. We were gathered at Sano's house in Berkeley. A long sword hung on the wall. He wanted to cut open his stomach. His eyebrows were flames, his eyes rapturous lakes. His mouth was a hole, and with his hands in fists and his bones about to shatter, he looked on the verge of eating himself. He ran out the door up the driveway to the road, where he stalked back and forth among the oaks, eucalyptus, and pines. He was out of scale, dwarfed by the slope, yet a giant against the sky. The world was open. But he was trapped on a ledge. From the hole he expelled Japanese, a language he had determined, years before, to swallow, and had swallowed.

The first recorded act of ritualized suicide was committed by a poet in twelfth-century Japan. The poet was trapped, with his sons, in a temple, Byodo-in, in Uji, Kyoto. Arrows were screaming past their ears. The poet was also a warrior— poet-warrior or warrior-poet, maybe neither is emphasized. No hyphen, therefore the sanctification of both halves. His name was Minamoto no Yorimasa. The Heike were advancing upon the temple. Yorimasa tore up the wooden bridge spanning the moat. The Heike, undeterred, rushed forward on horse and foot. Yorimasa was struck in the right elbow by an arrow. An arrow struck his younger son, Kanetsuna, under his helmet. His oldest son, Nakatsuna, was killed.

Samurai, facing death, believed that to commit *seppuku* would uphold their honor while depriving the enemy of power over their death. It became part of their responsibility to their clan, themselves. Yorimasa's suicide, though not the first in Japanese history—preceded by a score of anonymous samurai—was performed with such finesse it served as a model of the noblest way to take leave of the world.

Yorimasa wrote a farewell poem on the back of a fan:

> *Like an old tree*
> *From which we gather no blossoms*
> *Sad has been my life*
> *Fated to bear no fruit*[35]

Midori was angry. He did not want to die. He ran to the top of a mountain. The mountain was more having to die but not dying. He was, on the ledge, facing what was very soon going to erase the last possibility to do something, say something, be an active part of his own disappearance. He wanted to turn back. Turning back was the anger. Facing forward was the transposition of anger into oblivion.

He kicked June in the leg when she tried to bathe him. Water was too hot or too cold or felt foreign or bottomless. He pushed his son. He threw himself onto the red clay of North Carolina. The sword gleamed its ancient fish-symbol. You have carried yourself above the red clay, the water, but now you see me and must have me. I will give myself to you, but first you must eat me. That was the first penetration of the world that

35. Stephen Turnbull, *The Samurai Sourcebook* (London: Cassell, 2002).

would not stop moving. How old did he feel? He inhaled the oaks, eucalyptus, and pines. They were not his home. He was not on the ledge, not facing any direction, but spinning. I was standing at the bottom of the hill, watching a man becoming a monster.

Kimata Shimoda was among the last generation of samurai, Yumi Taguchi said. The Shimoda family was part of the feudal elite during the Tokugawa Era. During the Meiji Restoration, the family received a financial settlement, which they invested in a market. No one had experience running a market or even a business. It failed. *What was left was poverty and pride*, June said. (*There's so much pride*, she said.) By the time Midori was born, the samurai had long been extinct. The philosophy continued, in culture and myth, down through the family. Midori was the inheritor of a nationalism that manifest as family values. The samurai shone through holes in the archetypal shell, a codependent light by which everyone was drafted into descendancy.

*Midori had hard times especially in school,* June wrote, of Midori's second childhood in Seattle. *He couldn't speak English, so he was picked on for years. The Japanese pupils of the school Midori went to* [Bailey Gatzert Elementary] *were very lucky to have 'Miss Mayan'* [Ada Mahon], *a teacher who attached herself to the Japanese students and taught them pride in being Japanese.*

*There used to be so much pride that it oftentimes got in the way,* June said. *But, it helped Midori survive the things he had to go through— going to jail, being trailed by the FBI. Pride, and his self-esteem, you know, kept him going.*

> *He would always say,* What's the worst that could happen?
> *And I would say:* They could shoot you.

Midori told June that if he ever became so sick or infirm that he could no longer take care of himself, she was to shoot him. They did not own a gun, and there is no way she would have put her hands on one. I get as far as imagining June shooting at a bank of fog, missing.

One evening, when Midori was a teenager, he went to his girl-friend's house for dinner. It was his first time meeting her parents. It was a pleasant, unremarkable evening. A week later, Kawaki received a letter from the girl's parents. They wrote how happy they were to have Midori for dinner and also welcomed him, as their son-in-law, into their family. Kawaki was confused. Who were these people? She turned to Midori and asked, *What did you do? I had dinner,* he said. In the letter the girl's parents reiter-ated—revealed—that their invitation to Midori for dinner was also an invitation to marry their daughter. The girl was an only child. Her parents wanted a boy to bear the family name. They expected Midori, upon marrying their daughter, to change his last name. Midori did not know this. The girl had said nothing about it. Kawaki, feeling humiliated and betrayed, told Midori to go behind the house, cut his tongue out, and die.

Shortly after he killed himself, Yukio Mishima began appearing in his friend Yasunari Kawabata's dreams. Three hundred nights in a row.

*Legend, if we can already speak of legend, tells us that the last pages of the fourth volume,* The Decay of the Angel, *were written by Mishima on the very morning of November 25, 1970, a few hours, that is, before the end. The claim has been disputed: one biographer assures us that the novel was completed in Shimoda, a seaside resort where each year the writer spent the month of August with his wife and*

*two children. But to finish the last page of a novel does not necessarily mean that this book is done.*[36]

Kawabata composed, alongside his novels and short stories, even shorter stories, some less than a page, which he referred to (in English translation) as: *palm-of-the-hand stories.* Parts of some stories, in content or theme, enjoyed a second life in his novels. Other stories were afterimages or echoes of stories he had already written. He wrote "A Sunny Place" in 1923. It is the story of a young man who meets a young woman by the sea. She sees him staring at her and confronts him. Ashamed, the young man, averting his eyes, notices *a sunny place on the beach suffused with the autumn sunlight* and is returned to his youth, to the time after his parents died, when he lived with his grandfather, who was blind and spent all day sitting in the same place in the house, facing east, turning his head only to face south. To the south, the young man says, was *a sunny place.* The young man looks at the young woman again and, carrying with him the memory of both the young woman and his grandfather, yearns to *go out to the sunny place.*

*I went on shore early this morning (April 22) and walked up the large valley to the woods north east of Simoda. I found a great variety of flowers. In ascending the mountain by a very steep path, I passed a stone quarry neatly worked, and in a ravine above it, saw several new and interesting flowers. I went on shore (April 24) opposite the ship, and walked two miles around the Bay to Simoda, finding only a few flowers. From Simoda we walked up a small valley to the south west, over hills and valleys for several miles and found new flowers*

36. Marguerite Yourcenar, *Mishima: A Vision of the Void*, translated from the French by Alberto Manguel and Marguerite Yourcenar (Chicago: University of Chigago Press, 2001).

*everywhere. I found several new flowers in a long walk on the tops of the mountains and in descending to Simoda. I found a few plants, but after walking four miles (May 3), we were stopped by the rain in a poor village. Here the people may suffer from poverty, but if so they are the first that we have seen in Japan. They treated us very kindly and gave us shelter from the rain, and soon offered us tea and boiled sweet potatoes. I got a few more seeds and took a walk in search of flowers—perhaps the last time (May 11) before going to sea.*[37]

37. James Morrow, *A Scientist with Perry in Japan: The Journal of Dr. James Morrow* (Chapel Hill: University of North Carolina Press, 1947).

## THE INLAND SEA

When I think about Midori's degenerating brain, two images come to mind: a brain being overtaken by lush green vegetation, and an empty jar. I enter the jar. My intrusion echoes. I am at a loss, incapable of knowing what I missed. I walk around the lush green vegetation. It has transformed the brain into a small mountain. Impassable, full of shadows. The overlapping of a million leaves. Thick, snake-like roots. White trumpet flowers, indigo, lime. When I get close, the insects hold their breath. The flowers close. Mist.

The lush green vegetation and the empty jar are ruins. One evacuated. One overgrown. Both abandoned. Each concealing, within abundance or emptiness, a mind I believe is still intact, still capable of generating thought, but in submission, suppressed by the weight of what is overgrowing, what has been taken away.

Midori went for a walk. He walked into the trees. He wanted to touch them. He touched them. They did not feel the way they once felt. They felt coarser, cold. The higher up the trees, the darker, and the higher up the sky, the darker, and the darkness swelled. Faces grew out of the swelling. Midori had always gone to the trees for companionship, consolation, but now the trees were hostile. Especially in the evening. Their faces, contorted and mocking, grew shadows, long, and the longer they grew, the more they grew into one indivisible shadow.

One morning, Midori opened the door of June's sedan, climbed into the front seat, and released the parking brake. The car rolled backwards down the driveway. Across the road, the neighbor's grass, a bank of mud, into the lake. June noticed Midori was not in the house. She looked out the kitchen window. The car was gone. She ran outside. She could see the car half-submerged in the lake. She ran down the driveway, across the road, the neighbor's grass, the bank of mud. She ran into the lake. Midori was staring through the windshield, his hand on the brake. When he released it, the house became smaller.

Midori was born and died on the Inland Sea. Though I attributed a greater spiritual weight to his death, I attributed a greater spiritual gravity to the Inland Sea in Japan. Translucent islands, a horizon through which the water became sky and sun, and the birthplace of my ancestors. The Inland Sea in North Carolina was a lake. Not exactly profane, but it did not strike me as mythological. June and Midori lived on Lakeshore Drive across from the Inland Sea for thirteen years. The Inland Sea was the glorification of what was more commonly referred to as Lake Norman. It had been excavated and poured in the early 1960s, and named after Norman Locke, president of Duke Power Company. The water from the Catawba River, contained by a dam, was stocked with silver bass, bluegill, yellow perch, rainbow trout, and turtles. Denver, North Carolina, a main street of nondescript businesses, churches, banks, mobile home lots, new and used, was originally called Dry Pond, after a puddle of water on the northwestern edge of town that appeared every spring and dried out every summer.

The last time June entered a body of water was seventy years earlier, when she rescued her younger brother Saburo from the irrigation ditch. Until the morning Midori rolled the car down the driveway, she had not gone into the lake. Nor had she touched it with her foot. She stood in the lake to her thighs. The car was facing up the hill. Neighbors stood in the grass. Everyone knew June and Midori. They were good people, and Midori had Alzheimer's. Plus, they were Japanese. At the time of Midori's death, Denver had a population just above 10,000. 96% of the population was white, 3% black, all other ethnicities, including three Japanese Americans—Midori, June, Risa—making up the remainder.

A neighbor telephoned June to tell her that Midori was walking down the road in his underwear. He *moved his bowels in a basket*, June said, so she lined the wastebaskets with plastic. Once, when June was making cookies, Midori took the bag of chocolate chips and put it in the dryer. He tried to force open the sliding glass door onto the back patio. He shook the door. June locked it in place with a metal pin. Midori shook the door and the pin popped out. She let him sit in the driver's seat of their car, parked in the driveway, so that he could pretend to drive, to feel like he was going somewhere.

There was water in the car. June forced open the door and said to Midori, *You're all wet.*

Even into old age, June referred to her dead brother Jay deferentially as her older brother. He would always be the one who came first. His body was pulled out of the ditch, hauled into the house, attempts to save him were late, he was buried in a small box. For June, every body of water was the irrigation ditch. It was less the water then what was hidden in it. Because what was hidden in it, which she was not going to enter the water to confirm, was what had taken her older brother Jay, and almost her younger brother Saburo.

*185*

Kappa are supernatural creatures that live in water. They have reptile faces, turtle shells, a halo of hair, webbed fingers and toes. They lure humans into bodies of water to drown them. They drown them to eat their livers. It is believed that there is a magical ball at the mouth of the asshole called shirikodama. Some kappa lure children into water in order to eat their shirikodama. The mind goes there. And must sometimes stay, to prevent what sounds legendary, or simply outrageous, from manifesting, coming true.

Midori was the first Alzheimer's patient at Abernethy, the assisted-living facility where he spent the last years of his life. The patients were permitted access to an enclosed patio. Midori collected rocks and placed them on the outside sills of the patients' windows. He was not aware of who or what was on the other side. Not patients, or people, but each rock had a personality, formed against the backdrop of time, which appeared as an ocean or a desert: rocks rising out of water, water evaporating to rocks. One was always measuring the space, the vastness, of the desert and the ocean against rocks. And though the rocks became larger and larger, they were becoming smaller and smaller. Midori was sympathetic to the rocks that were small. He could see largeness in a small rock. Each was singular and self-contained, despite being drawn from the immeasurable mass.

There comes a point, with all the rocks picked up and placed on windowsills, when there are no longer any rocks on the ground. That is the point when the rocks are moved one sill to another, which is not arrangement or rearrangement, exactly, but the vibrating skin of the horizon.

After Midori died, June threw his negatives away. His photographic negatives, comprising nearly the whole history of his life as a photographer. She put them in a garbage bag and carried them out to the driveway, where they settled into the darkness of their wishful grace period, waiting to be rescued, reclaimed. But there was no one to question their absence. June figured photographs existed as photographs. The photographs on the walls, in the cabinets, spiral-bound albums, mounted on cardstock, dispersed among their children and grandchildren. Negatives were, if anything, drafts, attesting to work that no longer had use.

The garbage bags must have felt like leaves. Where was the transfer station, the landfill? It felt (still feels) like Midori's work, commingled with garbage, had been cursed by the same force that took over his brain, both dragged, helplessly, into the pit.

We did not talk about it. Our silence was surrogate for forgiveness. We imagined, in our grief, that the negatives were not, in fact, thrown away, but still existed, that it was all just a misunderstanding. That they were misplaced. Because if June did not know what negatives were, maybe she did not know, for sure, whether or not she had thrown them away.

He could have gone on forever. Maybe Midori and June had decided—conspired—years before, to draw the fruits of his vision, and their time together, into an ultimately invisible space, leaving only a few photographs to grow into the public, familial monuments, by which all of the others, the unborn, the negatives, would be remembered, more specifically, forgotten.

In the eighth of Akira Kurosawa's dreams, a traveler visits a village whose main attraction are its watermills.[38] As the traveler enters the village, a group of children brush past him. They stoop down in the grass to pick flowers. Richly colored, everywhere. They place the flowers on a stone.

The traveler encounters an old man with white beard and straw hat mending a waterwheel by hand. He asks the man about the village. *It is a nameless village*, the old man says. *But outsiders call it: The Village of the Watermills.*

The tourist asks the man why the children were putting flowers on the stone. *A very long time ago*, the old man says, *an ailing traveler fell dead on that spot. The villagers took pity and buried him right where he died. They placed that rock there as a kind of tombstone and offered flowers to it. It became a custom that continues to this day. It isn't just the children*, the old man continues. *All the villagers put flowers there as they pass.*

The traveler hears a jubilant sound coming from the other side of the river. *Is there a festival today?* he asks. *No*, the old man says, *that's a funeral.* The traveler looks confused. *You seem to find that odd*, the old man says. *But a funeral is actually a joyous occasion. All the villagers gather to carry the dead to the graveyard on the hill. The lady being buried today is ninety-nine. In fact, I must go now and join the procession*, he says, getting up. *To tell you the truth, she was*

38. Akira Kurosawa, *Dreams*.

*my first love. But she broke my heart and married another guy,* the old man says, then starts laughing.

The old man disappears into a house and emerges wearing a red smock and holding a bell rattle. He picks a spray of scarlet flowers and waits for the funeral.

The funeral procession appears on the path through the woods on the other side of the river. Children, throwing flowers, lead the procession. There is music and singing and dancing, people in straw hats with colorful streamers. There are drums and horns, a large man playing a tuba. In the middle of the procession is a coffin, covered with a colorful cloth, being carried on the shoulders of several people. When the procession crosses the river, the old man joins the children, and the procession continues.

The traveler watches. After the procession passes, he crosses a wooden footbridge to a stretch of land in the middle of the river, picks a handful of yellow flowers, crosses back over, and places the flowers on the stone. Long grass waves in the water.

*I knew a young boy named Midori. He seemed frail, like the apricot flowers extending their branches from the garden to the roadside. Because he had just come out of the isolation ward. The navy blue smell of his new clothes stings my eyes. Suddenly it grazed my eyes. He is running into the dim orchard. Screaming. It sent animal-like reverberations everywhere. Bare white feet floating in space. In the end the boy never came back.[39]*

**The last time I saw Grandpa was shortly before he died. It was in the nursing home and he had succumbed to most of what Alzheimer's**

---

39. Chika Sagawa, "Dark Summer" in *The Collected Poems of Chika Sagawa* (Ann Arbor: Canariam Books, 2015), translated from the Japanese by Sawako Nakayasu.

*took from him by then. I can't remember much from that day, and most of what I remember isn't really about him, but I have three moments of memory from what was probably a short visit. I remember walking down the hallway to his room—it was long and light but also seemed like a tunnel or a bubble, so separated from the rest of the world. Then I remember standing on the side of Grandpa's bed, as he sat upright, with a sheet over his bottom half, staring straight ahead, and attempting to eat or drink some food with difficulty. He didn't recognize me although he hadn't in a while, but it was the first time that it seemed like he'd really left his body—like Grandpa was gone and it was just his body (barely) functioning. I remember looking past him toward the door and just wanting to walk out of it—not wanting to see that life for him anymore. And then I remember exiting the doors of the nursing home, back into the rest of the world and thinking how I'd probably never see him again.*[40]

---

40. Kelly Shimoda, in an email, May 12, 2018.

## THE TEMPLE OF THE GOLDEN PAVILION

At two-thirty in the morning on July 2, 1950, Hayashi Yoken, a twenty-two year-old monk, set fire to Kinkakuji, the Temple of the Golden Pavilion, in Kyoto. He held a match to a small bundle of kindling he placed near a wooden portrait of Ashikaga Yoshimitsu, the temple's founder. Hayashi Yoken was going to burn himself with the temple but at the last minute lost his nerve and ran into the woods. He ran to the nearest mountain, Daimonji. He watched the Golden Pavilion burning through the trees, the fire reflecting in its pond. He downed a bottle of sleeping medicine, then stabbed himself in the heart. Some said he had been stricken by the temple's beauty. Some said he despised its ostentation. Some said he wanted to take it away from the people who came to defile the relics of the Buddha with their gawking. Some said he was a paranoid schizophrenic. Some said he had dementia. His mother said he was short-tempered and shy.

He confessed. *I used paper and mosquito netting to start it, and after seeing the fire catch, I ran away and drank sleeping medicine I had bought one week previously. Although I had planned this from the time I made the purchase, even now I do not believe I have done anything wrong.*[41]

---

41. Albert Borowitz, *Terrorism for Self-glorification: The Herostratos Syndrome* (Kent, Ohio: Kent State Universtiy Press, 2011).

The Golden Pavilion was five centuries old. By four in the morning, it was gone. Firefighters were able to rescue Yoshimitsu's portrait but with its head blackened and badly deformed. Yoshimitsu was the first patron of Noh. He funded the Noh actor Zeami Motokiyo, who was much younger, and with whom he fell in love. One of the monks remarked that Hayashi Yoken never had a girlfriend. His knife missed his heart. He had stab wounds beneath his left collarbone. A fire alarm had recently been installed in a small room on the first floor of the Golden Pavilion, but it stopped working and had been sent out to be fixed.

焼失後の金閣寺　昭和25年7月2日

If Hayashi Yoken burned the Golden Pavilion because of its beauty, whether its beauty was overwhelming or unbearable, why did he stab or try to stab himself in the heart? If the Golden Pavilion was going to die, so was he, but he did not want to die. Instead, he downed sleeping medicine. To consign his pain to sleep, to his unconscious? Did he not want to feel the pain of the burning pavilion?

Before seeing the Golden Pavilion for the first time, Mizoguchi, the Hayashi Yoken-inspired protagonist of Yukio Mishima's *The Temple of the Golden Pavilion*, imagines it as both *a small, delicate piece of workmanship* and *a huge, monstrous cathedral that soared up endlessly into the sky.*[42] The reconciliation of the two forms the basis for Mizoguchi's obsession.

The Golden Pavilion was rebuilt in 1955. Hayashi Yoken, sentenced to seven years in prison, released after five, died a year later.

It was a clear hot summer day in Kyoto. Hundreds of people passed before the Golden Pavilion. The trees were animated, in waves, with cicadas. Large, straggling tours trailed tour guides, old women, whose voices floated over the brown and green pond. The tourists were either extrapolations or betrayals of Hayashi Yoken. It was difficult—watching the people stare longingly, absent-mindedly, or not even raise their eyes—to tell the difference between reverence and disinterest, disrespect. They were not, in their minds, watching it burn.

Lisa and I stood in the trees. The pavilion, covered in gold leaf, concentrated the sun, refined it into a skin. The golden phoenix on the roof, wings raised, tail feathers fanned out, evoked the memory of Hayashi Yoken's fire. A white heron picked its way across the small rock island in the pond. The Golden Pavilion stood, over the edge of the pond, like a monument to the elegance of insular grieving. Sealed in gold, it simultaneously absorbed, repelled, and controlled the sympathies of the people, wherever people could, in the pavilion's untranslated cosmology, be said to exist. I expected a door to slide open.

---

42. Yukio Mishima, *The Temple of the Golden Pavilion*, translated from the Japanese by Ivan Morris (Rutland, VT: Charles E. Tuttle, 1956).

A young mother and father and their young daughter, three or four, stopped on the path before the Golden Pavilion. The mother was holding the girl. The girl was struggling, trying to wriggle free of her mother's arms. Her mother put her down. Neither she nor the father spoke. They signed to each other. The daughter stared up at them, watching their hands. Then she spoke, in a quiet voice—the quiet of someone talking to herself in a room. Her parents responded in sign language. The mother was Japanese. The father was white. They were deaf. The daughter was not.

Watching the young girl with her parents, I thought of my father. *I can hear birds, sometimes water,* he said, the last time I saw him. That was almost a decade ago, years after he stopped speaking to my sister, a few years before he stopped speaking to me. He was in the process of moving from the United States to Laos. He is, as I write this, alive, and exists as a knot in the throat of these final pages. The reasons why I have not spoken about him, not directly, until now—in the moments before departing this book—exist in the same unresolved fog with the reasons why he stopped speaking to my sister, then me.

My father's name is Midori Shimoda. He is Midori's second son, the only one of Midori's children who was there when he entered Abernethy, and the only one of Midori's children who was there when his body was cremated. He rarely spoke about his father—the unresolved fog surrounds the bridge connecting my grandfather and me—though they were close, had always been close, despite the last decade, during which he watched his father become anguished and unpredictable, paranoid and abusive, mindless and hollow.

*I am profoundly deaf in one ear and on the border of severely and profoundly deaf in the other*, my father said. I knew, when I was growing up, that he was *hard of hearing* (the phrase we used), but I did not know what that meant, not exactly. He rarely, if ever, talked about it, and when he did, he was elusive. Or, I could not *hear* it. Only that there was a time every night when his hearing aids came out, and sat like snails on the sink. That was when he disappeared, and I knew not to talk to or try to engage him. It did not occur to me that he might have looked forward, every day, to the moment when he took his hearing aids out, and that when the moment arrived, he experienced the most extraordinary relief.

The third floor of the Golden Pavilion is empty. The wooden floor is polished, a dark mirror. It perpetuates a soundless vortex that haunts the temple grounds. Even the old women, and the people straining to hear them, are drawn into the empty room, where their voices resolve into a single crystallophonic tone and drop straight through the mirror. The woman who stands with strangers in front of a wall and talks about camellia blossoms knows more than anyone that the flowers are saving themselves for the unborn, that what the living see is a rehearsal.

Years after my family left the house where I grew up, I returned to it. The neighbors' house had burned down. I walked through the ashes. I had not known my neighbors well. They were an older couple, with grown children. I have a vague memory of their youngest daughter, Tina, who was, when we were very young, our babysitter. The vague memory is of Tina, with blonde hair, green sweatshirt and jeans, standing at the end of our driveway, waving. The ashes were black. And produced, in complete disarrangement, the skeletons—appliances, furniture, stairs—of the neighbors' house. A photograph of a young woman standing before a fireplace was half-buried in the ash on what was once the fireplace's mantel.

Then I walked through the trees. I went up the front steps and rang the bell. The door opened onto an empty hallway. A young girl with blonde hair, no more than four years old, appeared. She was just tall enough to reach the doorknob. She looked up at me. I looked down at her. *Have you seen anyone in my room?* I wanted to ask. *Have you followed anyone into my room?* Her eyes were enormous. But she did not look scared. Behind me stood a row of tulip trees, then gray birch, thousands, interminable, forming a wall. *Or . . . have you seen anyone strange, or unfamiliar, going up the stairs?* I envisioned the girl in what once was my room. I envisioned her drawing a flower on the wall (the sky, an ancient, limitless monument). Starting with a line. The line curving. Then adding a shadow. A flower, like a face, mistaken for the being (what is recalled, what is remembered). Then adding an ear, many ears. Eyes. I envisioned the girl staring at the eyes on the wall and asking of the eyes, *Do you recognize me?*

A woman's voice came from around a wall. *Who's at the door?* The girl did not answer. Her mother appeared. I realized, or felt, that I was trespassing. *I used to live here*, I managed, suddenly unsure. *I wanted to visit.* The woman asked if I wanted to come in. Her invitation startled me. I did not know how to answer. I thought, for a moment, that maybe I was a ghost, and that part of being a ghost, was being invited into the house where I used to live, so that I could follow my ghost predecessors, including my grandfather, up the stairs, into my room, and into the wall. *No*, I said, *I just wanted to see.* See what? I had not seen anything. I thanked the woman, then the young girl, who, even as I walked away, into the trees, continued to hold the door open.

The last time I saw my grandfather, his face came off the wall. I was young. Kelly and I were visiting our grandparents in North Carolina. We were getting ready for sleep, our sleeping bags side-by-side on the carpet in front of the fireplace. The fireplace was cold. A wind descended, blew through the room (the Inland Sea). Then our grandfather entered from down the hall, our grandmother (a rectangle of light) calling behind him in a soft voice. She was trying to get him into the bath. I could hear the water running. He was wearing a blue and white yukata. He walked toward us, until his feet touched our feet. Then he looked down. His face was a mask. I could see, through the holes in his mask, startled lakes, and the still-living earth of his face. What I remember most clearly is that he did not have teeth. His mouth was a black hole, lips sucked in, rushing backwards through his face.

I had never seen my grandfather without teeth. A simple thing, but it felt, in that moment, like a violation. Not that he was violating us, but we were violating him. With our naiveté, fear. We were in his house, on his floor, catching him in a private moment, before the bath, in which he was taking himself apart. I was struck with the thought that my grandfather was dead. That he had already died, and had been replaced by a toothless apparition, who was as frightened—of us, of the world that produced children, vaguely familiar permutations of himself—as it was frightening. The old man standing above us was not real. That following the removal of his teeth, every part of him could be taken off or out—his limbs, his nose, his eyes, his heart—leaving behind not a man, not my grandfather, but a shelf, more specifically an altar. An altar from which all the relics and offerings had been removed, an altar waiting to be populated, fulfilled. My grandmother was calling him, *Midori-san, Midori-san*, but she never appeared. She never caught up. The hallway was as long as a lifetime.

I used to have a dark brown papier-mâché mask. The mask was a ghoul's melting face, grotesque and suffering: long pockets of skin, a long arched nose with deep nostrils, long eye sockets. I remember once my grandfather putting it on. And even though we watched him put the mask on, and even though we knew the mask was mine, and were not disturbed when I was the one putting it on, we were scared. There was, because I could not see his face behind the mask, no guarantee that he had not been replaced by someone else—with or without a face of their own—who might overstep the boundary the mask was testing.

On the wall behind my grandfather was a photograph, black and white, that he had taken, lifetimes earlier, in Monument Valley. It was enlarged, floor-to-ceiling. It was the most prominent of his photographs, not only because it was the largest—what felt like the dimensions of Monument Valley—but because it occupied the largest wall in every house where my grandparents lived—from the house where they raised their children, to the house in North Carolina. It was a photograph of a land before time. Sandstone buttes, mounted on pyramids of rock, were pedestals from which the busts of gods had been removed, or disintegrated. Clouds, above the buttes, were white dresses, gilded by a soft, matriarchal sun. The bottom of the photograph was sand and brush. The valley carved out of the buttes and the arc of clouds created a circle, filled with light, in the center of the photograph, which looked—while I was falling asleep, staring with what light came through the window—like an eye, at first, then an egg. My grandfather, standing above us, had walked directly out of it. Directly out of the desert. Directly out of the wall. He had come an extraordinary distance. He had come magnificent distances. Was he in search of someone, something? Whomever or whatever it was, he had reached, instead, his grandchildren. Our feet, a naked stream at the edge of the desert, were small and white, yet flowing.

I was just learning how to see. I fear I have not learned fast enough. The aureole was luminous but bare. It was a place that held my grandfather once, a place, between monuments, out of which my grandfather had come, the desert he made rising behind him.

## PHOTOS AND IMAGES

Wooden chairs in Oko (Brandon Shimoda)

Kawaki Okamoto, Hiroshima (photographer unknown; Shimoda family collection)

Kawaki Okamoto (photographer unknown: Shimoda family collection)

Still of Sumiko Kurishima from Mikio Naruse's *Every-Night Dreams* (Shochiku Company Limited)

Death Valley (Brandon Shimoda)

Yamato (Midori Shimoda)

Brandon and Kelly Shimoda, Beatty, Nevada, 2011 (June Shimoda)

Kawaki Okamoto Shimoda with her sons Makeo, Setsuo, Yoshio, and Midori, Hiroshima, 1910s (photographer unknown; Shimoda family collection)

A page from the Kumamoto phonebook (Brandon Shimoda)

Okiku (by Hokusai & Yoshitoshi)

Geiichi Shimoda, 1950s (Midori Shimoda)

United States Ship *Finback* (Lyold B. Everton)

*Africa Maru* (Walter E. Frost)

Detail of *Photographers Using Non-silver Processes* (Center for Creative Photography, Tucson, AZ)

Setsuko Shimoda, 1930s (Midori Shimoda)

Setsuko and Midori (photographer unknown; Shimoda family collection)

Midori Shimoda in the Peace Park, Hiroshima, 1983 (June Shimoda)

Door in Domanju, Hiroshima, 2016 (Brandon Shimoda)

Brandon in Kumamoto, 2011 (Lisa Schumaier)

Midori Shimoda, Devon Hurst, and friends, Bluff, UT, 1940s (photographer unknown; Shimoda family collection)

Midori in Mirror, Fort Missoula, 1943 (Peter Fortune, Peter Fortune Memorial Collection, courtesy of the Historical Museum at Fort Missoula Collection)

Midori Shimoda, Fort Missoula, 1943 (Peter Fortune, Peter Fortune Memorial Collection, courtesy of the Historical Museum at Fort Missoula Collection)

Midori and friends, Seattle, 1920s (photographer unknown; Shimoda family collection)

Untitled photograph (flower, New Jersey, 1960s) (Midori Shimoda)

Midori at House of Camellia, Tokyo, 1983 (photographer unknown)

Samurai on a poster in Nagasaki (Brandon Shimoda)

Mishima family in Shimoda (Eikoh Hosoe)

Midori on the beach (photographer unknown; Shimoda family collection)

Midori Shimoda in Kanazawa, 1983 (June Shimoda )

June in smoke, Denver, North Carolina (Kelly Shimoda)

June and Midori, 40th wedding anniversary (photographer unknown; Shimoda family collection)

Midori Shimoda's baby photo (photographer unknown; Shimoda family collection)

Golden Pavilion, 1950

Midori and Dori Shimoda, Dumont, NJ, 1950s (Midori Shimoda)

Monument Valley (Midori Shimoda)

## TEXTS

Permission to reprint email correspondence throughout has been given by Hiromi Ito, Karen McAlister Shimoda, Kelly Shimoda, and Risa Shimoda. Permission to reprint passages from Hiromi Ito's poetry has been given by Hiromi Ito and her translator, Jeffrey Angles. Permission to reprint a passage from Chika Sagawa's "Dark Summer" (translated from the Japanese by Sawako Nakayasu) has been given by Canarium Books (thanks to Joshua Edwards and Lynn Xu). Permission to reprint excerpts from Tomoe Otsuki's "Reconstruction of 'Christian City Nagasaki' in Postwar Years" has been given by Tomoe Otsuki. Permission to reprint the edited transcript of Richard Potashin's interview with Margaret Stanicci has been given by Densho (Seattle, WA).

# INSPIRATIONS AND ACKNOWLEDGMENTS

*The Grave on the Wall* is the title of this book as well as all the books—cannibalized, misplaced, forgotten—that came before it, out of which this one unfolded. I began writing *The Grave* in 2010. It began as a meditation on the photograph of my grandfather wearing a bra and slip (Fort Missoula, 1943), then expanded and contracted, at various points (every point), into a straightforward (however fragmented) biography of my grandfather, meditations on the desert, glacial lakes, the immigration of Japanese picture brides to the United States, the atomic bombings of Hiroshima and Nagasaki, the incarceration of Japanese immigrants and Japanese Americans during World War II, the sun, hell. Each, one after the other, evaporated to reveal, in the elongating stains of their memory, old women, flowers, mirrors, shadows, ghosts, and long, unabridged passages from my favorite books. I have felt, throughout all the above, the loss—the losing—of my grandfather and the guilt of contributing to his being lost. I have also felt the clarifying, the enshrining, of our relationship, and an understanding of being a grandchild.

Some part of all that remains.

*The Grave* would not have been possible without my grandmother June and my aunt Risa. They have, for many years, been extremely patient and forthcoming in answering my questions, even when I have asked the same question innumerable times, often without explanation. Some of *The Grave* is in my grandmother's voice. I have included throughout passages from her journals, an interview I conducted with her in 1999, and conversations since. Risa, who is the bearer of our family's history, has done a phenomenal amount of research—including reclaiming my grandfather's FBI file—and has traveled great distances, in putting her father's story together.

The following is a partial list of works—books, essays, short stories, movies—that inspired, motivated, and sustained the writing of *The Grave on the Wall*. (The sources of quoted texts are cited throughout the book either in footnotes or the body of the text.) I have always imagined the perfect book would consist of nothing but passages and images drawn directly, and without abridgment, from the works of others, arranged in no particular order: Etel Adnan, *Sea and Fog.* James Baldwin, *No Name in the Street.* Roland Barthes, *Camera Lucida* (tr. Richard Howard). Jorge Luis Borges, "The Aleph" (tr. Norman Thomas Di Giovanni). Theresa Hak Kyung Cha, *Dictee.* Don Mee Choi, *Hardly War, The Morning News Is Exciting.* F. Hadland Davis, *Myths and Legends of Japan.* Dot Devota, *MW: A Field Guide to the Midwest.* Louis Fiset, *Imprisoned Apart: The World War II Correspondence of an Issei Couple.* Vilém Flusser, *The Freedom of the Migrant.* Lafcadio Hearn, "Some Thoughts about Ancestor Worship," "Jikininki." *The Tale of the Heike* (*Heike Monogatari*) (tr. Hiroshi Kitagawa and Bruce T. Tsuchida). Yasushi Inoue, *Chronicle of My Mother* (tr. Jean Oda Moy). Inujima Seirensho Art Museum, Inujima, Japan. Hiromi Ito, *Killing Kanoko, Wild Grass on the River Bank* (tr. Jeffrey Angles). Bhanu Kapil, *Ban en Banlieue, Incubation, Schizophrene.* Yasunari Kawabata, *Palm-of-the-Hand Stories* (tr. Lane Dunlop and J. Martin Holman). Maxine Hong Kingston, *The Woman Warrior.* Masaki Kobayashi, *Kwaidan. The Kojiki: Records of Ancient Matters* (tr. Basil Hall Chamberlain). Akira Kurosawa, *Dreams.* Youna Kwak, *The Second Life. Man'yoshu* (Collection of Ten Thousand Leaves). Yukio Mishima, *The Temple of the Golden Pavilion* (tr. Ivan Morris). Malika Mokeddem, *Century of Locusts* (tr. Laura Rice & Karim Hamdy). Kristin Prevallet, *[I, Afterlife] [Essay in Mourning Time].* Amarnath Ravva, *American Canyon.* Robert J. Smith, *Ancestor Worship in Contemporary Japan.* Natsume Soseki, *The Three-Cornered World* (tr. Alan Turney). Rea Tajiri, *History and Memory: For Akiko and Takashige*. Ivan Turgenev, "Kasyan from the Beautiful Lands" (tr. Richard Freeborn). Carol Van Valkenburg, *An Alien Place: The Fort Missoula, Montana, Detention Camp 1941–1944*. Simone Weil. *The Need for Roots* (tr. Arthur Wills). Karen Tei Yamashita, *Letters to Memory*. Kunio Yanagita, *About Our Ancestors: The Japanese Family System* (tr. Fanny Hagin Mayer and Yasuyo Ishiwara).

*The Grave* is part of a family of books that includes *Lake M* (Corollary Press, 2010), *O Bon* (Litmus Press, 2011) and *Evening Oracle* (Letter Machine Editions 2015). Some of the passages here are enlargements of feelings first expressed in poems in each of these books.

To the editors of the following journals, who published passages from *The Grave on the Wall: Entropy, Evening Will Come, Fanzine, Harriet* (Poetry Foundation), *The Margins* (Asian American Writers' Workshop), *The Massachusetts Review, Nat. Brut, The Offing, P-Queue*; especially Allison Cardon, Lawrence-Minh Bùi Davis, Janice Lee, Tony Wei Ling, Jyothi Natarajan, and Joshua Marie Wilkinson; to the individuals and organizations who guided me through my research, especially Densho (Seattle), Sharon Garner (Fort Missoula Historical Museum), Ruth Okada, Tomoe Otsuki, Richard Potashin (Manzanar); especially Margaret Stanicci; to my friends and guides in Japan: Isao Aratani, Baba-san, Zana Cohen, Shoso Hirai, Sumiko Hirosawa, Yoshie Honda, Yasumasa Imamura, Yutaka Iwasaki, Mayumi Kondo, Keijiro Matsushima, Keiko Ogura, Ryohei Shirai, Shotaro Yoshino; especially Mihoko Furuya, James Jack, Hiromi Ito, and Keiko Shirai; to the Arizona Commission on the Arts, Millay Colony for the Arts, and Santa Fe Art Institute, for time and space; to the countless people who offered their homes to stay and write in, for nights, days, weeks, sometimes months; to my friends who challenge me with their curiosity, their humor, their insights, their brilliance, and the ongoing example of their work, especially those who inspired both general and specific parts of this book; especially Elisabeth Benjamin, Youna Kwak, Molly McDonald; to Sesshu Foster, Myriam Gurba, and Bhanu Kapil, for the generosity of their work; to Etel Adnan, Don Mee Choi, Wong May, Rea Tajiri, and Jeffrey Yang, for their encouragement and example; to everyone at City Lights: Chris Carosi, Stacey Lewis, and especially Elaine Katzenberger; to my family: Teri Akashi, Joy Endow, Susie Fukuhara, William Fukuhara, Frances Agena Shimoda Harris, Neil Harris, Winnifred Elizabeth Shimoda Harris, Alan Kuramoto, Setsuko Kuramoto, Kawaki Okamoto, Geiichi Shimoda, June Shimoda, Karen McAlister Shimoda, Kathi Shimoda, Kelly Shimoda, Midori Shimoda, Risa Shimoda, Yumi Taguchi, Asano Yamashita, Saburo Yamashita; and especially to Lisa Schumaier and Yumi Taguchi Schumaier Shimoda,

Thank you.